It's A Matter Of Faith And Life
Volume 2

A Catechism Companion

The Apostles' Creed
The Lord's Prayer

David M. Albertin

CSS Publishing Company, Inc., Lima, Ohio

IT'S A MATTER OF FAITH AND LIFE — VOLUME 2

Copyright © 1997 by
CSS Publishing Company, Inc.
Lima, Ohio

All rights reserved. No part of this publication may be reproduced in any manner whatsoever without the prior permission of the publisher, except in the case of brief quotations embodied in critical articles and reviews. Inquiries should be addressed to: Permissions, CSS Publishing Company, Inc., P.O. Box 4503, Lima, Ohio 45802-4503.

Scripture quotations are from the *Revised Standard Version of the Bible*, copyrighted 1946, 1952 ©, 1971, 1973, by the Division of Christian Education of the National Council of the Churches of Christ in the USA. Used by permission.

Some scripture quotations are from the *Holy Bible, New International Version*. Copyright © 1973, 1978, 1984 International Bible Society. Used by permission of Zondervan Bible Publishers. All rights reserved.

From Luther's *Small Catechism*, 1986, Copyright 1986 Concordia Publishing House. Used with permission.

"Seven Stanzas at Easter" from *Collected Poems* 1953-1993 by John Updike. Copyright © 1993 by John Updike. Reprinted by permission of Alfred A. Knopf Inc.

Library of Congress Cataloging-in-Publication Data

Albertin, David M., 1939-
   It's a matter of faith and life / David M. Albertin.
     p. cm.
   Contents: v. 1. Baptism, confession, absolution, the office of the keys, and holy communion — v. 2. The Apostles' creed and the Lord's prayer — v. 3. The Ten commandments.
   ISBN 0-7880-0356-9 (pbk. : v. 1). — ISBN 0-7880-0357-7 (pbk. : v. 2). — ISBN 0-7880-0358-5 (pbk. : v. 3)
   1. Luther, Martin, 1483-1546. Kleine Katechismus. 2. Lutheran Church—Catechisms—English. I. Title.
BX8070.L8A7   1997
238'.41—DC21
                                        96-47408
                                            CIP

To my three children
Timothy
Jonathan
Kristen
and their children

Table Of Contents

Preface	7
The Apostles' Creed: First Article Creation	11
The Apostles' Creed: First Article God The Father	17
The Apostles' Creed: First Article Our Care Of God's World	23
The Apostles' Creed: Second Article Who Is Jesus?	31
The Apostles' Creed: Second Article What Did Jesus Do? Prophet, Priest, And King	39
The Apostles' Creed: Third Article The Holy Spirit	47
The Apostles' Creed: Third Article The Holy Spirit — Comforter And Counselor	55
The Apostles' Creed: Third Article The Church	61
The Apostles' Creed: Third Article The Forgiveness Of Sins ... Resurrection ... Life Everlasting	69
The Lord's Prayer: Introduction To The Lord's Prayer	77
The Lord's Prayer: The First Petition	85
The Lord's Prayer: The Second Petition	91
The Lord's Prayer: The Third Petition	99
The Lord's Prayer: The Fourth Petition	105

The Lord's Prayer: The Fifth Petition	113

The Lord's Prayer: The Sixth Petition	119

The Lord's Prayer: The Seventh Petition	125

Preface

It's A Matter Of Faith And Life originally appeared in the form of a script for a television program (*The Lutheran Lexicon*) which appeared on the Michigan City, Indiana, ecumenical community access cable channel. It also has been employed in the catechetical instruction of junior high youth at Immanuel Lutheran Church of Michigan City.

In its present form *It's A Matter Of Faith And Life* appears as a narrative companion to Dr. Martin Luther's *Small Catechism*. It is written in a style that should be attractive to readers of all ages.

Each chapter of *It's A Matter Of Faith And Life* focuses on a part of the *Small Catechism*. For example, there is a chapter on Baptism Part One, the Second Article of the Apostles' Creed, the Third Commandment, the Fourth Petition of the Lord's Prayer, and so forth. Each of these chapters does not exhaust the content of what the Catechism has to say. Rather the chapters focus on a key and significant issue that underlies the particular part being discussed.

It's A Matter Of Faith And Life, this book of words about words which ultimately focuses on the Word, can be employed as a devotional reader or as a supplement to the Catechism in catechetical instruction. The biblical quotes have been taken from the Revised Standard Version of the Bible. Some of them, however, are my own liberal translations and summaries. The references to the *Small Catechism* have been taken from the 1986 edition of *Luther's Small Catechism With Explanation*, Concordia Publishing House, St. Louis, Missouri.

The material in *It's A Matter Of Faith And Life* reflects my five decades of being a Christian. These pages began to be formed by the influence of my parents and the church which I attended as a child. The many references and examples cited have been gleaned from my childhood experiences, the Christian instructors at whose feet I have sat, my own reading and studying, and from what I have encountered as an adult and a pastor. Therefore, precise documentation and citing of sources is frequently absent. Instead, I would like to thank all of those who have had an effect on my Christian formation: my parents, my Sunday School teachers, my various instructors at the three Concordias I attended, and my friends both on the "street" and of the academic.

In other words, this is a book about life, the life of a Christian, and how the six chief parts of the Christian faith as presented in the *Small Catechism* of Dr. Martin Luther interacted with his life and gave shape and direction to it.

God be thanked for the numerous and wonderful ways He has provided for my Christian pilgrimage and growing in the faith. These pages have been written to share with you some of that which has been shared with me.

Soli Deo Gloria

David Albertin
Michigan City, Indiana
Winter 1996

The Apostles' Creed

The Apostles' Creed: First Article
Creation

Imagine a time before the "beginning." Actually that is impossible, because time is a "ruler" (a measuring device) that shows the relationship between things. Therefore, there is no "time" before the beginning, before there are things. Also, do you remember from science class the old rule of the universe: "You can not add to or subtract from matter"? Thus the universe of ours is a "closed system." Now imagine, if you will, God calling into being "matter." Once God has all this "matter" on His hands, what do you suppose He had to do with it? Yes, the first challenge that faced God at this time, now that there was time, was to organize all this "matter." How would you have gone about it, about organizing it? What would you have done first, second, and so forth?

❖ ❖ ❖ ❖ ❖

At the beginning God created the heavens and the earth. The earth was without shape or form ... But the Spirit of God was present over this primordial chaos.

And God said, "Let there be light." And there was light. And He separated the light from the darkness. And it was good.

And God said, "Let there be sky in the midst of all of this chaos." And so God made the sky, and it divided the waters above from the waters below. And God called the sky "Heaven."

And God said, "Let all the waters under the sky be gathered together into one place, and then let dry land appear in the midst of the waters." And He called the dry land "Earth." And the gathering of the waters He called "Sea."

And God said, "Let the earth bring forth grasses and herbs and trees."

And God said, "Let there be lights in the sky to divide the day from the night; and let them regulate the days, and the seasons, and the years." And God made two great lights; the greater was to rule the day and the lesser one was to rule the night. And it was good.

And God said, "Let the waters bring forth many living creatures." And so He created the fish and the whales and the birds. And it was good.

And God said, "Let the earth bring forth living creatures, each after its own kind: cattle and creeping things, and all sorts of beasts."

And finally God said, "Let us make man in our own image, after our own likeness. Let him have charge over the fish of the sea, over the birds of the air, and over the cattle of the earth." So God created man in His own image. Yes, man was created in God's image.

And God saw everything that He had made, and behold, it was very good. Therefore, on the seventh day God ended His work and He rested.

Such a cosmic fugue.

What a wonderful orchestration.

A magnificent symphony.

Oh, the majesty of creation and the wonderment that it inspires. "The heavens declare the glory of God, and the firmament showeth His handiwork."

A fugue is a musical composition that begins with one theme that is repeated and developed by different voices or instruments. A symphony also is a musical composition that blends together many voices or instruments that develop a theme. What theme do you hear or see in creation? Could it be one of order in distinction from confusion? If so, what are the implications of that?

A number of years ago a traveling exhibit of the artwork of Claude Monet, the famous French impressionist, toured the United States. I distinctly remember viewing it. And I remember what I said as I stood in a room surrounded by his glorious paintings of the lily pads at Giverny, his home in France not too distant from Paris. I said, "This is like the first day of creation, and the second and the third and the fourth, fifth, and sixth." He had put so much color into the universe of his canvass that it staggered the imagination, just as one's imagination is staggered as he or she beholds with an appreciating eye the majesty of God's handiwork. Lie on your back on a moonless but starlit night and gaze at those stars and beyond. Once you have done that you will never forget it.

There are many ways in which one can admire creation. 1) Gaze into the sky on a starlit night. 2) Visit a planetarium. 3) Go to the art museum. 4) Look at a drop of pond water under a microscope. 5) Investigate a corner of your yard. 6) Stand on a mountaintop or at the seashore. 7) Stare into a flower. What impression does such an activity give you? Give expression to such an impression. What is your favorite "view" of creation?

Or simply marvel at a drop of pond water under a microscope. You will discover there is another universe that you did not even know existed. All of that inspires us all to become psalmists: "The heavens declare the glory of God, and the firmament showeth his handiwork."

Nevertheless, it is very easy to get a good argument going when it comes to the subject of creation. Creationists (those who say that God created the world and the whole universe) and evolutionists (those who say that all that we see is the product of some "natural" process of evolution) love to go round and round about it. It is interesting to note, however, that the Bible is not really that interested in proving that God created this universe and all universes beyond. For the biblical man of faith there never was any question about matter's Maker. It was just accepted that the hand of

Creationists and evolutionists are often at odds with each other. Make two (side by side) lists of the Order of Creation, one according to the Bible and the other according to the evolutionists' view. Compare their similarities and differences.

God was behind it all. What was the issue, however, was man's response! That response first and foremost was and is to be a response of wonderment and awe. It is a response which leads to hymns of praise, much like Francis of Assisi's paraphrase of Psalm 148:

Be praised, my Lord, with all your created things.
Be praised for brother sun, who brings the day and gives us light. He is fair and radiant with a shining face, and he draws his meaning from on high.

Be praised, my Lord, for our brother wind, and for the air and clouds and calm days and every kind of weather by which you give your creatures nourishment.
Be praised, my Lord, for our sister water, which is very helpful and humble, precious and pure.
Be praised, my Lord, for our brother fire by which you light up the darkness; he is fair and gay and mighty and strong.
Be praised, my Lord, for our mother earth, for she sustains and keeps us, and brings forth all kinds of fruits together with the grasses and bright flowers ...
Be praised, My Lord, for all your creatures.
We give you thanks.

Such a posture of praise also has a humbling effect on us. We realize that a tremendous gift has been given to us for which we are to care. And we might wonder, "Why?" Why has God given it all to us? The Psalmist, in awe of creation and humbled by the honor given to him and to all people, the honor of caring for God's masterpiece, leads us in saying and singing:

O Lord, our Lord, how majestic is thy name in all the earth.
Thou whose glory above the heavens is chanted by the mouth of babes and infants,
thou hast founded a bulwark because of thy foes, to still the enemy and the avenger.
When I look at thy heavens, the work of thy fingers,
what is man that thou art mindful of him, and the son of man that thou dost care for him?
Yet thou hast made him little less than God, and dost crown him with glory and honor.
Thou hast put all things under his feet,
all sheep and oxen, and also the beasts of the field, the birds of the air, and the fish of the sea, whatever passes along the paths of the sea.
O Lord, our Lord, how majestic is thy name in all the earth! — Psalm 8

Why has God given the universe to us? What are we to do with it?
What are we to do because of it?

America's past poet laureate, Robert Frost, once said, "It's a glory!" And to think it is ours. Mere words suddenly become inadequate....

Questions

1. What is a "creationist"?

2. What is an "evolutionist"?

3. Are there ever any points of contact between the two of them?

4. What is the Bible's chief concern with regards to our reaction to creation?

5. Why did God give it all (creation) to us?

Discussion

1. Discuss the nature of a "fugue."

2. Have you ever experienced awe when observing the work of an artist? Share your experience and relate it to creation.

The Apostles' Creed: First Article
God The Father

❖ ❖ ❖ ❖ ❖

Creeds (they can be either formal or informal) give expression to what people think is true. The two most well-known creeds in the church are the Apostles' Creed and the Nicene Creed. They are formal. The Declaration of Independence can also be considered a creed. "We believe these truths to be self-evident...." These words also are formal. What we believe to be true also gives direction to our behavior, our actions. What are some of your creeds? Give expression to what you believe to be true. Some of these expressions might be very informal. How do these creeds affect what you do?

Some people say that what we need are "fewer creeds and more deeds." What do you think?

❖ ❖ ❖ ❖ ❖

"I believe in God, the Father Almighty, Maker of heaven and earth." With those words we join with the church throughout the centuries and in all places confessing and giving witness to our faith in God who is the creator of this universe and of all universes beyond.

With those words we also begin the Apostles' Creed. We call it the "Apostles'" Creed not because the Apostles were its authors, but rather we call it that in honor of them and, more importantly, in honor of the faith which they have bequeathed as an inheritance to the church throughout all these centuries.

We call it the Apostles' "Creed" because the word "creed" refers to an expression of something that is believed. The word comes from the Latin word *credo*, which simply means, "I believe." Thus, when we together say the words of the Apostles' Creed those words are our witness to the world of what we believe. Those words are a witness of faith that we share, which we have in common, with Christians who live around the world and who have lived through all those centuries since Christ walked on this very earth.

So, let's get on with this creed!

We begin at the beginning, with the First Article of the Creed. It focuses our attention on the beginning, the beginning of time, and upon Him who is the very creator of time. We call Him "God the Father." I confess that "I believe in God the Father Almighty, Maker of heaven and earth."

Martin Luther in the *Small Catechism* writes these words of explanation:

> *I believe that God has made me and all creatures; that He has given me my body and soul, eyes, ears, and all my members, my reason and all my senses, and still takes care of them.*
> *He also gives me clothing and shoes, food and drink, house and home, wife and children, land, animals, and all I have.*
> *He richly and daily provides me with all that I need to support this body and life.*
> *He defends me against all danger and guards and protects me from all evil.*
> *All this He does only out of fatherly, divine goodness and mercy, without any merit or worthiness in me.*
> *For all this it is my duty to thank and praise, serve and obey Him.*
> *This is most certainly true.*

Rewrite in your own words Martin Luther's explanation of the First Article of the Apostles' Creed. What are some of the direct effects these words have on how you live your life?

I suppose that when we think of God "the Father" our first response is to think of Him as the Almighty Creator, He who by His might and power set everything in motion. That is perhaps the most universal concept of God that there is. When we think of God, we think of creation. All the parts of the universe around us point to that. The Lord God has made them all. "All things bright and beautiful, all creatures great and small. All things wise and wonderful. Yes, the Lord God has made them all."

What are some of the ways in which God demonstrates His power? Make a list of these ways, ranging all the way from the formation of new galaxies to new life coming from tiny seeds to miracles of healing

to words spoken in His name which give comfort. Does God really work through words? How did He call into being that which appears in Genesis 1? What are some other manifestations of His word? What good have your words done today? What harm have your words done today? Even as words are the most powerful demonstrations of God's power, words are the most powerful demonstration of our power. What does that mean for how we live?

In his explanation of the words of the First Article, Martin Luther acknowledges that He who is the creator, who is the prime mover of all things, is also the One who continues to provide, defend, guard, and protect what He has made. We call this "the providential care" of God. He who is the One behind the wind and the wave is the One to whom we turn when rain is needed, or in time of trouble, or when danger is at the door. It is almost like a natural instinct to do that. For instance, haven't you heard it said many times when all else has failed, "Well, all we can do now is pray"? In a sense that simple expression is a confession that God is still there, that God still has the power, and that God is still in control.

So far all of that sounds rather reasonable. It is rather logical. One doesn't even have to be a Christian to agree with it. But what follows now is the unique Christian insight that Luther's Explanation to the First Article of the Creed gives to us. Do you remember these words: "All this He does out of fatherly, divine goodness and mercy"?

Luther was very sensitive to the fatherly qualities of God which are presented to us in the Scriptures. For example, the ancestors of Jesus the Christ were called "the children of Israel." The prophet Hosea wrote, speaking for God, "When Israel was a child, I loved him, and out of Egypt I called my son." Jeremiah, also a prophet, spoke of "the Son of God, the Son of the heavenly Father." And in one of our hymns we confess as we sing, "Children of the heavenly Father, safely in His bosom gather. Nestling bird nor star in heaven, such a refuge e'er was given."

Our creator God then is not known and confessed as some almighty power which can at that moment just blow us over. God is not some impersonal force that has no concern or consideration for His creatures. No! We call Him "Father." I'd like to tell you a little love story which illustrates this. It is a story which I am sure the Father has told many times in many ways.

I don't think anybody really realizes how much I loved my son, my boy "Izzy." I had my heart set on him even before he was born. How delighted I was when I first set eyes on him. How excited I was when I dreamed of all the things we'd do together.

I remember one such moment. I'll never forget it. It happened one beautiful late fall Saturday afternoon. We didn't have anything to do, so my Izzy and I decided to go for a hike. We set off in the direction of the old railroad that used to run just down the hill from where we lived. Oh, how I remember the incident well. I decided to take Izzy by the hand. He was only five years old and had that habit of running here and there, sometimes without being too careful about where he was going. So, since he was still such a little guy. I thought it safest to hold onto his hand tightly so that he wouldn't wander off and get into any kind of trouble. Well, the sun was exceptionally warm that day, and all the chill from the night before melted beneath its brightness. Even the cold rails of the tracks warmed up quickly. So we walked down those tracks for a ways. I held on to Izzy's hand so that he would not slip or fall — for as I remember, that was the first time he had ever walked down the tracks of a railroad.

We felt good, side by side. I still remember the wires alongside the tracks humming. That's a sound you don't hear much anymore. But I remember it clearly. And those birds! How they sang. It was just as if they had one more, one last, beautiful song to sing before winter made its appearance.

On and on we walked, delighted by the babbling of a clear brook that flowed alongside the tracks and entertained by jack-in-the-box grasshoppers and darting jackrabbits. We were even amused by silly looking toads that sat on old, moldy tree branches which laid in the water and by the bees that buzzed overhead.

About four o'clock in the afternoon it happened. All of a sudden, for some unknown reason, my son pulled his hand from mine and ran down the little embankment on the side of the track. He went straight for the woods. I guess he was chasing a squirrel. At any rate, without looking, he took off running even though he had never been in the woods by himself before. I called to him, but he just kept on running.

I hurried after him as fast as I could go. But, well, the brush in the woods was just too thick. Soon I had lost him. I didn't know where he was going. I didn't know where he was. I called and called, but there was no answer. After what seemed like an eternity, I looked at my watch and saw that it was getting late. The sun was about to set. Soon it would be pitch-dark in that woods. That's when I decided that I could not give up. I would have to keep on looking. And sure enough, soon it got really dark. When in the woods, the sun seems to slip beneath its western horizon so quickly. And then there suddenly was no more light at all. No more warmth.

All the pleasantness and good feelings of the afternoon were gone. It was cold and dark. The playful little animals of a few hours before now became frightening shadows in the forest. Every little sound sounded big enough to scare you right out of your skin. Hours went by. I often felt like giving up, but I didn't. I couldn't. I kept calling and calling.

Well, my story has a happy ending. Along about midnight I heard a strange whimpering sound coming from beneath a tall pine tree. Could it be? Yes, it was! By the light of the moon that had risen high in the sky I saw my boy! I had found him! He didn't hear me approach. He was so worn out and so bruised from falling over stumps in the dark, so cut up from crashing into thorn trees. I reached down and picked him up and held him ever so close. I had found my son! Oh, how happy he was to see me. I held him close to my heart and carried him home.

That little story presents to me the image of the God of the First Article of the Apostles' Creed who is not just (yes, I would like to say "not just") an all-powerful creator God, and also who is not just a providential God, but who is our loving and caring fatherly God, and who picks us up and holds us close to His heart even though because of our own folly we have run off on our own and have fallen down bruised.

❖ ❖ ❖ ❖ ❖

God is also powerful as a Father. What are some of the powerful fatherly ways in which God has revealed Himself to you? Would you consider that to be another version of the "Izzy" story? Try your hand at writing your own "Izzy" story.

❖ ❖ ❖ ❖ ❖

Yes, "I believe in God the Father, the Almighty Creator, who has made me and all creatures. He provides for me, guards, protects, and defends me" and even calls me by my name — calls me by His very own name.

Questions

1. Why is the Apostles' Creed called by that name?

2. What is a creed?

3. Why is it important for us to remember the "fatherly" qualities of our creator God?

4. What was Izzy's basic problem?

Discussion

1. Can you think of any story which parallels the one about Izzy and his father? If so, share that story with others.

2. Discuss the "fatherly" qualities of God. Perhaps you might also like to talk about His "motherly" qualities.

The Apostles' Creed: First Article
Our Care Of God's World

If God had wanted us to fly, He would have given us wings.

(I'm not quite so sure.)

If God had wanted us to walk on the moon, He would have put some of us up there to begin with.

(I'm not quite so sure.)

If God had wanted us to ride around in automobiles, He would have put wheels on the end of our ankles instead of feet.

(And so the argument goes on without end, sometimes arriving at the strangest of conclusions.)

❖ ❖ ❖ ❖ ❖

Just for fun, dream up some other whimsical "If God had wanted us to … He would have …" statements. Most of these are probably tongue-in-cheek and are not to be taken too seriously like those referred to on this page.

❖ ❖ ❖ ❖ ❖

Now why in the world do you suppose that I said such silly things as I just did; that, for example, if God wanted us to fly He would have had us born with wings and so forth? Permit me to explain.

The last time we met, I discussed with you the words from the Apostles' Creed: "I believe in God the Father Almighty, Maker of heaven and earth." At that time I presented to you an argument, not at all silly, which speaks to us of our Creator God who is known to us as a very fatherly person. Yes, God is all-powerful, but He does not squash us under His thumb. Instead, to us He is as one who very carefully provides for us and who tenderly and lovingly looks after us. Indeed, He holds us in His arms, close to His fatherly heart.

Now let's talk about our response to God as creator and in particular about our response to what He has created. First, let's focus on God's good gift of this world, how we handle it, what we do with it, and how we care for it. To help us do that, let's turn to the *Small Catechism* once again. It will give us some direction and plan for our adventure.

Martin Luther explains the First Article of the Apostles' Creed this way:

> *I believe that God has made me and all creatures; that He has given me my body and soul, eyes, ears, and all my members, my reason and all my senses, and still takes care of them.*
> *He also gives me clothing and shoes, food and drink, house and home, wife and child, land, animals, and all that I have.*
> *He richly and daily provides me with all that I need to support this body and life.*
> *He defends me against all danger and guards and protects me from all evil.*
> *All this He does only out of fatherly, divine goodness and mercy, without any merit or worthiness in me.*
> *For all this it is my duty to thank and praise, serve and obey Him.*
> *This is most certainly true.*

The concluding words of this explanation are the ones we are interested in at this point: "For all this it is my duty to thank and praise, serve and obey Him." Let me ask you: "In what better way can we thank and praise, serve and obey God with respect to His world, His creation, than to take good care of it?"

Responding to what God has made and knowing what to do with it (caring for this world) is no whim. It is serious business. What are some of the potential consequences of not taking care of this world? How serious do you think these problems could become? Might humankind even go so far as to make human life impossible on this planet? What do you think are the prospects of maintaining life in space? On other planets?

In Genesis 1 we find the account of God creating the world, indeed, the entire universe. He did it in six days, however long or short those days may have been. The important point is that on the sixth day, the last day of creation, and after everything else had been made and put into order, we are told that the Lord God made man and woman. We are told that He made them "in His own image ... In the image of God He created them; male and female He created them." And then He said to them: "Be fruitful and multiply, fill the earth and subdue it; and have dominion over every living thing that moves upon the earth."

❖ ❖ ❖ ❖ ❖

God said, "Be fruitful and multiply and fill the earth." Do you think the earth is now full? Does this issue have anything to do with the concern over birth control? Does "subduing the earth" and having "dominion" over it have anything to do with the size of the human population? What are some of the suggestions that are often made regarding the control of the population? Which, if any, of these suggestions are acceptable to you?

❖ ❖ ❖ ❖ ❖

What do you suppose it means that we are made in the image of God? And what does it mean that we have been given the assignment of having dominion over the earth and that we are to subdue it? It simply means that we are to care for this world. We are to represent God here. We are to be stewards of all the natural resources that have been created by the Almighty. We are to take care of them as carefully as He would if He were standing here among us.

❖ ❖ ❖ ❖ ❖

What are some of the ways in which God has been portrayed? What are some of His images? Consider the work of artists, filmmakers, and storytellers. What kind of image of God do you have in your mind? J.B. Phillips in his book *Your God is Too Small* said that to some people God is like a policeman or a grand old man, or someone handy to have around because he can fix most anything. What kinds of images of God do some of the people you know have?

❖ ❖ ❖ ❖ ❖

To be in the image of God, then, does not mean that we are "look-alikes." There would be some mighty big problems if the image of God mentioned in Genesis 1 meant that we looked like God. If it did, what in the world would we do with maleness and femaleness, with whiteness and blackness, with shortness and tallness, and so forth? Instead, to be created in the image of God means that we are to have control over the created order of things, even if that control means flying through the air or walking on the moon. Yes, science and advancements in technology are part of our society, and, properly employed, can help us better be God's stewards of all the elements He has created.

❖ ❖ ❖ ❖ ❖
What are some of the ways in which God wants you to be like Him? Does this have anything to do with taking care of this world? If you were God's adviser, would you recommend that He turn the care of this world over to someone like you? If "yes," why? If "no," why?
❖ ❖ ❖ ❖ ❖

We live in a world, however, the reality of which tells us that often we do not do such a good job of living in this image of God in which we were created. We, for example, terribly abuse our environment. We pollute; we mistreat the countryside, the atmosphere, and our natural resources. And in addition to that, we often just don't do anything. We are just plain lazy when it comes to "subduing the earth" and having the kind of dominion over it with which God has charged us.

Water, air, and ground pollution are big problems these days. Make three lists and identify ways in which the water, air, and ground are being polluted. Now identify some of the polluters and their pollution. For example, pollution is caused by industries, communities, and individuals (like yourself).
❖ ❖ ❖ ❖ ❖

It can and should be said by us that there simply is never any justification for the wanton waste of natural resources. That is true, however, not just for fear that we might someday run out of this or that. (In our first science classes in school we learned that immutable law of physics which says that you "cannot add to or subtract from matter.") Yes, we may eventually wear out some form of matter, but the substance of a thing will always turn up in another form. True, we might someday run out of some mineral or the other — perhaps gold or oil — but there will always be something to take its place, although what takes its place might not be as helpful for life as that which has become exhausted. So the issue here is not some catastrophe if we run out of some sort of mineral (resource) or the other, as great and as serious as that catastrophe might be. The issue is: Respect! Respect for all of God's creation, because that respect also reflects our respect for the Creator. Therefore, the question is: How do we treat this gift from God, the whole gift, in whatever form we find it?

What are some steps that can be taken to stop all this polluting? Be specific. What can industries, communities, and individuals do? One of the biggest problems we have is with waste disposal. What can be done with all our waste (garbage)? How can we cut down on the amount of waste (garbage)? What do you personally plan to do? Be specific and set a schedule for doing this.

> Respect is a big and important issue in life. Besides doing something about pollution, what are some other ways in which you can show respect for this "created order of things"? What, also, are some of the ways in which you can show respect to the Creator?

❖ ❖ ❖ ❖ ❖

If someone gave you a masterpiece of art, I am sure that you would not keep it outside under the porch. If someone gave you a grand piano, I am sure that you would not leave it outside under a tree in the rain. If someone gave you a Mercedes-Benz, I don't think that you would use it as a garbage truck. So, also we should regard with respect all the natural resources of this world and the universe as priceless gifts from God.

❖ ❖ ❖ ❖ ❖

> Life, especially human life, is worthy of our respect. Discuss ways in which respect can be shown to people who are at various stages of life: for example, the unborn, the handicapped, the elderly, the disadvantaged, the people with whom you share your life. In this respect, consider also the "hot" issues such as euthanasia, adoption, living wills, welfare, and so forth. In each of these areas what kind of action to think is called for if it is motivated by respect?

❖ ❖ ❖ ❖ ❖

Of course, at the top of the list of gifts from God is the gift of human life. No human being ought to ever be treated carelessly or shamefully by another human being. For we are all created in the image of God; we all have dignity from God. And that has something to say about how we treat one another.

❖ ❖ ❖ ❖ ❖

> Is animal life and plant life to be treated differently than human life? If so, why? If not so, explain.

❖ ❖ ❖ ❖ ❖

When talking about life, we should also include the other forms of life which are abundant in nature. Wildlife. Animal life. Dogs, cats, and squirrels. Forests and grasslands. The Humane Society reminds us that we should be humane toward pets and other animals. To be humane means to be kind and considerate, to respect the right every living thing has to life, because life is a gift of God and is created by Him. And if we are in His image, then certainly it is through His eyes that we should look at everything which breathes and grows.

Sometimes we can associate creation with putting things in order. Is there any relationship between that idea and how we (you) keep our yards, our rooms, our lives?

Some people might say that if we left our hands off of things it would be a better world. They say that the best of all conditions is to let everything revert to its natural state. What do you think about that? Or do you think that it is important for people to be about the business of making this world a better place in which to live?

When we pollute and abuse, when we are careless toward creation, we participate in the process of reversing creation — if that is at all possible. What I mean is that in Genesis 1 God made everything, and He put it into order. He created a fine masterpiece of art out of chaos. He painstakingly put a star over here and a moon over there. Every blade of grass was assigned its place. Every drop of water was suspended just where it was supposed to be. It was called "an Eden, a Garden of Eden." But when we tear it down and throw it around we destroy what God has established. When we turn our back on the mirror of His image in which we were created, He shines through us no more.

Certainly what I have just said applies to polluting the air with soot or to pouring lethal chemicals into the water. But what I have said also applies to other rather commonplace experiences in life. Think of it this way: The next time you are ready to toss a soda pop can out of a car window, at that very moment every other human being on earth, all the billions of us, ought to have the right to toss a can, too. What a mess that would be. And the next time you leave a hamburger wrapper on the beach or throw a gum wrapper on the floor, think of it: Every other person in the world ought to have the right to do it, too. What a mess! Such a garbage heap! Obviously that is no way to care for God's world.

I think that you can see now that "to thank and praise, serve and obey" God, as the words of Luther's explanation to the First Article of the Creed instruct, means that created in His image we are to be faithful in caring for this world which He has given to us. It's old-fashioned language, but we are to be "stewards" of His gifts. In no better way can we recognize and confess God as Father — our Creator.

Luther says that "to thank and praise" God is also an important way for us to respond to what He has made. Produce, invent, construct some way in which you can do just that: "thank and praise God." Be specific. Fill in the detail.

Questions

1. What does it mean to be "created in the image of God"?

2. In Biblical language, what is a "steward"?

3. If you pollute, do you think everybody else has the right to do the same?

Discussion

1. Discuss some of the major ecological concerns facing us today. Include in your discussion ways in which we can respond and make a difference.

2. Some say that much of the concern about nature these days is often nothing more than a return to primitive nature worship. Comment on that.

The Apostles' Creed: Second Article
Who Is Jesus?

❖ ❖ ❖ ❖ ❖

In the last chapter you were asked to think some whimsical thoughts about how God could have created us (what He could have made us to be like). Now think whimsically again. If you could add your advice (like Martin Luther said he would have), what would you suggest that God do in order to save the world and us in it? What would be the strong points of your plan? What would be its weak points? What is the "genius" in God's plan? How is it superior to yours?

❖ ❖ ❖ ❖ ❖

Martin Luther wrote:

He puts a Babe in a crib. Our common sense revolts and says, "Could not God have saved the world in some other way?" I would not have sent an angel. I would simply have called in the devil and said, "Let my people go." The Christian faith is foolishness. It says that God can do anything and yet makes him so weak that either his Son had no power and wisdom or else the whole story is made up. Surely the God who in the beginning said: "Let there be light, let there be a firmament, let the dry land appear," could have said to the devil, "Give me back my people, my Christians." God does not even send an angel to take the devil by the nose ... He is helpless without his mother, and he suffers him to be nailed to a cross. The devil says, "I will judge him." So spoke Caiaphas and Pilate, "He is nothing but a carpenter," and then in his weakness and infirmity he suffered himself to be trodden under the foot of man and to be crucified, and through weakness he takes the power and the Kingdom." (The Martin Luther Christmas Book, Roland Bainton, Trans., Fortress Press, Philadelphia, 1948, pp. 47-48.)

Who is Jesus? In the *Small Catechism* this is what Martin Luther has to say about "Who Jesus is":

I believe that Jesus Christ, true God, son of the Father from eternity, and true man, born of the Virgin Mary, is my Lord.
At great cost He has saved and redeemed me, a lost and condemned person.
He has freed me from sin, death, and the power of the devil — not with silver or gold, but with His holy and precious blood and with His innocent suffering and death.
All this He has done that I may be His own, live under Him in His kingdom, and serve Him in everlasting righteousness, innocence, and blessedness, just as He is risen from the dead and lives and rules eternally.
This is most certainly true.

In many ways, we are best described and identified by what we do. What are some of the things for which you are known? What have you done with and in your life? What kind of "picture" of you does all of that make? Now make the following four lists and add details from the life of Christ as found in the four Gospels (Matthew, Mark, Luke, John): Teacher/Preacher; Miracle Worker; Revolutionary; Savior. What kind of picture of Him does that make? There are also other pictures and identifications of Christ. Some think that He is merely a product of people's imaginations, or that He was an angel or a phantom, or some special adopted son of God. What evidence from the four Gospels can you find for these ideas?

The question "Who is Jesus?" has drawn a lot of attention down through the centuries. And there have been all sorts of answers. For example, some people have said that He was a great moral teacher, or a worker of miracles, or a revolutionary, or even the figment of some people's imagination. Some have said that He was a special angel sent by God to the earth. Some have thought Jesus to have been "a son of God" much like you and I are sometimes called "sons" (and "daughters") of God. In such a case, the term indicates a special relationship but not one of "origins" or of "beings." It would be much like my calling some young fellow "son," but that would not make him the same as "my" son of whom I am the father. So, some have thought that Jesus was like an adopted son. Still others say that perhaps He really was a special spirit that took on bodily form — something like a phantom ... and so on.

When heroes die all sorts of exaggerations of their moral character and accomplishments seem to be developed over time. We have a tendency to make our heroes (sports, political, military, and so forth) better than what they might have been. Can you give any examples of

this? Do you think that this kind of thinking applies also to the person of Jesus?

❖ ❖ ❖ ❖ ❖

Confessing the words of the Apostles' Creed, however, we believe, teach, and confess that Jesus was not just another man who appeared on a troubled scene, felt that He must do something about it, paid for his efforts with His life, and then later was idealized by those who had become His disciples, and who, faced with His absence, were not able to live with just the memory of a dead hero. Thus, they invented all sorts of stories about Him and embellished what He had actually done with a lot of exaggerations.

❖ ❖ ❖ ❖ ❖

In respect to Jesus, the "die had been cast" a long time before He came to the earth. Identify as many Bible references from the Old Testament as you can which identify who Jesus was and what He would do. What did the Old Testament say about the nature and character of the One who would be the world's redeemer?

❖ ❖ ❖ ❖ ❖

No! We believe, teach, and confess that the person of Jesus is God Himself, who came to this earth of ours in order to fulfill and complete a plan of salvation for all of humankind, a plan which had its beginning already back with Adam and Eve — a plan which is the central message of all that history and prophecy recorded in the Old Testament scriptures.

❖ ❖ ❖ ❖ ❖

The snake is probably the world's most despised creature. Why do you think that is so? What are some of the "evil" ways that you can remember that the snake has been presented in art, in film, in literature? And yet why do you imagine that the snake is part of the Caduceus, the symbol of the medical profession? Read the curse that God put on the snake at the time of temptation in Genesis 3. Do you think that the snake had legs before this?

❖ ❖ ❖ ❖ ❖

Let's review a little bit of that record.

When Adam and Eve first sinned against God (we call that "the Fall"), these words were spoken by God to the devil, who had appeared in the form of a serpent and who had been successful in tempting Adam and Eve into sin: "I will put enmity between you and the woman, and between your seed and her seed; he shall bruise your head and you shall bruise his heel." Now, those words from Genesis 3 mean a lot more than just that someone is going to get his heel bitten in the process of stepping on the head of a snake. The "enmity" mentioned means that there is going to be a battle going on, and that battle is going to rage between Satan and a descendant of Eve. In the light of the New Testament we see that this is a prophecy (indeed, the first prophecy) of Jesus, and it is given way back there in the third chapter of the Bible.

Jesus often had to do battle against Satan. Refer to Matthew 4. We too have to do battle against Satan. Refer to Ephesians 6. What does this have to say about the power and presence of Satan? What does the conflict between Jesus and Satan have to say about who Jesus is?

❖ ❖ ❖ ❖ ❖

So it was that Jesus did do battle against Satan. And, yes, in the process He was bruised. He was crucified. But, also in the process, He crushed the head of Satan. He conquered death and rose again from the grave. That spelled defeat for the devil.

Thus you can see that already in the opening words of the Old Testament, we are beginning to get a look at just "who Jesus is." He is the One who did battle against the devil and won.

To be a "man without a country" is a terrible thing. To be "somebody" you must have a place to call your own. How important do you think that was in the telling of the Old Testament story? How important is that for the Incarnation of Jesus?

❖ ❖ ❖ ❖ ❖

There are other passages also from the Old Testament which continue to speak to us about who Jesus is. In Genesis 12, for example, God chose a man called "Abram," renamed him "Abraham," and told him that from his family, his descendants, would come a blessing for the whole world: One who would be a blessing for the whole world. So it was that Abraham had a son. His name was Isaac, and Isaac had a son whose name was Jacob, and Jacob had twelve sons, and they became known as "the Children of Israel." They were given the land of Canaan as a promised land. There their nation was established. There they had such kings as David and Solomon. To them all was given through the voice of the prophets that same promise that had been given to Adam and Eve

❖ ❖ ❖ ❖ ❖

There are some Messianic prophecies listed here. Can you identify any more? The use of a "reference" Bible or a concordance will help. But it will take some work and some effort. Look up such words as "prophecy" and "messiah." As you develop a list of prophecies, do you notice any trends or patterns that help you to identify who Jesus was/is? What

> are some of the significant things that are contained in these messianic prophecies?

❖ ❖ ❖ ❖ ❖

and Abraham. For example Isaiah said: "To you will be born a child ... To you a son will be given ... And the government shall be upon His shoulders, and His name will be called Wonderful, Counselor, Mighty God, Everlasting Father, Prince of Peace." This "Immanuel" ("God with us") will be born in Bethlehem, so wrote the prophet Micah.

❖ ❖ ❖ ❖ ❖

> The promise made to Abraham in Genesis 12 is reflected in the genealogical lists of Jesus found in the New Testament. Look at the one in Matthew 1. It follows the heritage of Jesus all the way back to Abraham. Luke 3:32ff takes the genealogy way back to Adam. The lists have some other differences, too. What might be a reason for that? Consult a commentary for an explanation.

❖ ❖ ❖ ❖ ❖

So, "Who is Jesus?" He is the One who is the fulfillment of all those messianic prophecies (promises of the Messiah) that kept on ringing out for thousands of years. These were promises of God's help and deliverance for a world full of a people in trouble.

Thus it was that "in the fullness of time," God sent forth His only begotten Son to be born of a woman, to be born of the Virgin Mary, in Bethlehem. But Jesus was different than all other infants born in Bethlehem or in any other place. He was different not just because His birth had been so long promised and so long awaited. He was different (and this is the important part) because as we believe, teach, and confess, He was also God, the second person of the Holy Trinity. In our creeds we now call Him "the Son of God."

Now, you might ask, "How is this possible that Jesus is both a son of man and the Son of God? How can He be both human and divine at the same time?" Well, quite frankly, that is a mystery. How could God be both in heaven and on earth at the same time? And even more astounding is this: If Jesus really is God, and He died, does that mean that God died, too? As you can see, those kinds of questions can go on and on.

❖ ❖ ❖ ❖ ❖

> What does it mean that Jesus was human, that He had a human nature? On the other hand, what does it mean that Jesus was divine, that He had a divine nature? Is this understandable according to the laws of nature? What does it mean to accept something by faith? What are some of the things in nature which you don't fully understand, but

which you accept by faith? What role do the Scriptures play in faith-building, in accepting things by faith? Are the Scriptures reliable? Can you depend upon what they say? What are some things that can only be accepted by having faith in what the testimony of the Scripture gives?

Nonetheless, we accept (we believe, teach, and confess) the testimony of the Scriptures on the subject, realizing full well that there are some things about which our minds will never completely know all the answers. Yet, the testimony stands: "In the beginning was the Word, and the Word was with God, and the Word was God ... And the Word became flesh and dwelt among us, full of grace and truth; and we have beheld His glory, glory as of the only Son from the Father" (John 1:1, 14).

John 1 talks in a majestic way about the "Incarnation." Be sure to properly define the word "incarnation." What do the words of John 1 tell us about the "Incarnation"? What detail do they give us?

Even though we don't always necessarily understand something, it is still necessary for it to be. In your own words explain why it was necessary for Jesus to be both God and man, divine and human.

Therefore, Christians speak of both the human and the divine natures of Jesus. Again, how can that be? I don't fully understand HOW that can be, but I do know WHY that had to be. In my catechism classes I tell my students that it was necessary for Jesus to be both human and divine for these reasons: He had to be human so that He could come down low enough to redeem us. He had to be one of us if His life on the cross was going to count for us. But He also had to be divine so that the sacrifice would be big enough to get the job done. Just another human on a cross would have been just another life wasted. You see, that life on the cross had to count for us all.

Write your own paragraph detailing who Jesus was/is. Write a word portrait of Him. Or if you can draw reasonably well, paint a picture of Jesus. However you picture Jesus, do it reasonably well. Why do you think that is encouraged?

So, who was, is, Jesus? He is the One of whom the Scriptures speak. He is the One who did battle against the forces of evil on our behalf. He is both God and man, human and divine. He is my Lord, our Savior, whose visit to this earth has made more difference than anything else that has ever happened in the course of human history.

Nineteen wide centuries have come and gone and today He (Jesus) is the centerpiece of the human race and the leader of progress. I am far within the mark when I say that all the armies that ever marched, and all the navies that ever were built, and all the parliaments that ever sat, and all the kings that ever reigned, put together have not affected the life of man upon this earth as powerfully as the One Solitary Life. ("One Solitary Life," author unknown)

Questions

1. If Martin Luther had been God, how would he have redeemed us from Satan?

2. Who is Jesus?

3. What is the first word of messianic prophecy in the Bible?

4. What messianic promises were given in Genesis 12?

5. What messianic promises were given in Isaiah?

Discussion

1. Discuss the significance of God redeeming us the way He did instead of doing it the way Martin Luther said he would have done it.

2. The human and the divine natures of Jesus are hard for us to understand. Discuss, however, why it was necessary for Jesus to be both God and man.

The Apostles' Creed: Second Article

What Did Jesus Do?

Prophet, Priest, And King

❖❖❖❖❖

The moral teachings of Jesus are among the most significant ever taught by anyone. Identify as many of them as you possibly can. Consider if they are important today. Some of them run contrary to popular opinion and there is a temptation to "water them down." Look at the Beatitudes (Matthew 5:3-12). How do these teachings run contrary to popular opinion? What are some of the ways that we often attempt to "water them down"?

Look also at some of the great parable chapters of Jesus' teachings (Matthew 13 and Luke 15). What do these parables mean as far as your life is concerned?

A parable is a story which reflects something that can be or can happen in real life. (The word means "to lay or throw something down alongside of something else.") Some parables help us to understand what happens in our own lives. The movies are often good examples of parables. They are not "real" but they reflect things that can "really" happen in our lives. Many of the Walt Disney movies are like that. Identify some of them and discuss how they are parables of real life.

❖❖❖❖❖

C.S. Lewis, a well-known Christian man of letters from England, once wrote: "I'm trying here to prevent anyone from saying that really silly thing that people often say about (Jesus): 'I'm ready to accept Jesus as a great moral teacher, but I don't accept His claim to be God.' " (C.S. Lewis, *The Case For Christianity,* Macmillan Company, New York, p. 45.) That's one thing that we must not say.

It is very easy for a person to content himself with identifying Jesus as "a great moral teacher," and even as a great worker of miracles. For example, we think of Him sitting on the slopes of those hills surrounding the Sea of Galilee teaching. The Evangelist Matthew has gathered together much of what Jesus said there and combined it into that section of scripture which we know as "The Sermon on the Mount" (Matthew 5-7). Add to those teachings the parables of the Prodigal Son, the Good Samaritan, the Rich Man and Lazarus and others, and you will have that for which Jesus is most famous to many people. He certainly was a great preacher and teacher.

In addition, He is often thought of as a miracle worker. No wonder: He changed water into wine at the Cana wedding. He walked on the waters of the Sea of Galilee. He healed and cured those who were blind, lame, and deaf. He even raised some people who appeared to be dead from the dead.

Identify as many miracles of Jesus as you can. In addition to showing the power and might and mercy of God, many of the miracles of Jesus have a secondary meaning which can be applied to our own lives. For example, Jesus stilling the storm can still the storms in our lives. Look at the list of Jesus' miracles that you identified. Look for ways in which those miracles speak to incidents within your own life.

Yes, these incidents from the life of Jesus are important. He did do marvelous things, and He did teach and preach like no one else ever had. When referring to Jesus doing and saying what He did, we speak of Him as a Prophet. A "prophet" is one who not only talks about things that are going to happen in the future, a "prophet" is also someone who stands up in front of (before — *pro*) people and speaks the life-giving and healing words of God. Jesus certainly was a prophet in that respect.

If Jesus was such a popular preacher and such a powerful worker of miracles, why do you suppose he never went into the public speaking or teaching business? Why do you think he did not set up a "tent" and advertise miracles of healing? Why do you suppose some people do that?

However, even more important than Jesus being a Prophet, He was a Priest. A priest in the biblical meaning of the word is one who makes sacrifices. Of course, when thinking of Jesus we know that He made the greatest, the most valuable, the most treasured sacrifice of all time when He willingly went to the cross of Calvary on our behalf. In the way that Jesus lived and gave His life we see that He truly was a "priest" for us.

That is why Martin Luther, after he had commented on "Who Jesus Is,"

I believe that Jesus Christ,
true God, begotten of the Father from eternity,
and also true man, born of the Virgin Mary,
is my Lord,

said these words in his explanation to the Second Article of the Apostles' Creed:

who has redeemed me,
a lost and condemned person,
purchased and won me from all sins, death, and the power of the devil;
not with gold or silver,
but with His holy, precious blood and with His innocent suffering and death.

That's what Jesus did! And that is the very heart of the Christian faith. To BE a Christian, then, is not just to believe in (let's say) "The Golden Rule," as good as the rule may be, and it is not merely exercising "The Good Neighbor Policy," as good as that policy may be. Rather, being a Christian is embracing Jesus, true God and true man, who suffered and died on the cross for the forgiveness of our sins, and who then rose again and now is living as our Lord eternally.

What is central to the Christian faith? "Embracing" what is central is something more than just knowing with the mind, as important as that is. "Embracing" also has to do with the heart. What does that mean?

No wonder then that the cross is the central object of the Christian faith. Go into any Christian church. Yes, there may be many symbols of the faith there. But one that will never be lacking is the cross. It reminds us of the most important thing that Jesus ever did for us. He died for us.

Symbols are "shorthand" for what they represent. For example, flags represent nations. Birds and animals often represent athletic teams. So also it seems that every religion has a symbol that represents it. Identify as many symbols of the world's religions as you can. Attempt also to understand what the symbols of these religions represent.

There are many ways in which the cross is presented. Sometimes it is with the body of Jesus on it; sometimes it is empty. There also are different shapes and designs of the cross. Draw some of them and then think about what the various shapes and designs mean.

There are also other symbolic items in most places of worship. Even the design of a building used for worship often has a symbolic meaning. Next time you are in your place of worship, identify as many symbolic items as you can. Consider also the purpose and function of these items.

❖ ❖ ❖ ❖ ❖

Make no mistake about it, His death was not just a charade. He literally died. We say that He gave Himself as a sacrifice to make atonement for us from the bondage of sin, death, and the devil. A price had to be paid. A ransom had to be made. Our hurtling headlong toward eternal death has been interrupted by Him who put Himself in our place. That's why we believe, teach, and confess that Jesus' death was not just a symbolic death. He did not just put Himself into a state of suspended animation for a few days. If that had been the case, then His resurrection would have been merely a resuscitation. And where would that leave us then with regard to our promised and hoped for resurrection? If Jesus had not been raised from the dead, then we have no hope of being raised from the dead.

❖ ❖ ❖ ❖ ❖

A symbol is not the real thing. It is only a representation. Why was it important that Jesus' death not be merely a symbolic death but a real one? In what ways was Jesus' death very real? What kind of death do you think yours will be?

❖ ❖ ❖ ❖ ❖

Yes, the cross reminds us of Jesus' death, and of the fact that His death was not pleasant. As the prophet Isaiah wrote many years earlier: "He was despised and rejected by men. A man of sorrows and acquainted with grief ... Surely He has borne our griefs and carried our sorrows, yet we esteemed Him, stricken, smitten by God and afflicted" (Isaiah 53). No wonder then that while on the cross He cried out as the blood trickled down His arms and from His forehead, His mouth parched as dry as you can possibly imagine, overwhelmed by pain and grief and exhaustion: "My God, my God, why have You forsaken me?" At that instant Jesus was claiming no divine privilege. He was dying. He knew it. And in His dying He was carrying the weight of the whole world on His shoulders.

Saint Paul in his letter to the Philippians records how the early Christians confessed this great truth: "(Even) though He was in the form of God (He) did not count equality with God a thing to be grasped, but emptied Himself, taking the form of a servant ... and became obedient unto death, even death on a cross" (Philippians 2:6, 7, 8).

In "Seven Stanzas at Easter" John Updike wrote of the reality of the death and subsequent resurrection of Jesus this way:

*Make no mistake about it; if He rose at all, it was as His body; if the cells' dissolution
did not reverse, the molecules reknit, the amino acids rekindle, the Church will fall.*

Then he goes on to say that Jesus' death and resurrection were not merely like the passing away of the flowers in the fall which reappear again in the spring as if they had only gone through a stage of dormancy. The death of Jesus is more serious than that. He died. Just as all people die.

❖ ❖ ❖ ❖ ❖

If Jesus' death was for real, so also is it important that His resurrection be real. Read the lines from Updike's poem. What do you think about what they say? What does that mean for your resurrection? How real do you think it will be? What do you think it will be like? You might want to read all of 1 Corinthians 15 in this regard.

❖ ❖ ❖ ❖ ❖

*His hinged thumbs and toes, his valved heart, which pierced, died, and began to wither
and decay and then, was gathered by the Father's might and brought back to life.*

Finally, Updike concludes:

*Let us not mock God with metaphor, analogy, sidestepping transcendence, making of
the event a parable ... Let us not seek to make it less monstrous.*
— "Seven Stanzas at Easter"

So it was that when Jesus had endured all that He could, He cried out with a loud voice, "Father, into Thy hands I commend my spirit." Then He gave up His very last breath of life and died.

That, however, was not the end of the story. That is not the end of the story. He was resurrected. He was restored to life by the power, by the creative power, of the Father. Therefore, Martin Luther concludes his explanation to the Second Article of the Apostles' Creed saying that Jesus did all of this so:

*that I may be His own and live under Him in His kingdom and serve Him in everlasting
righteousness, innocence and blessedness, just as He is risen from the dead, lives and
reigns to all eternity. This is most certainly true.*

Jesus as sacrificer and sacrifice on the cross is our priest; He is our High Priest.

❖ ❖ ❖ ❖ ❖

**What are some other words that could in various circumstances be
substituted for "Lord"? Some of these words might be positive in nature**

> and some might be negative: for example "leader" or "boss." If Jesus is Lord in and of your life, what are some of the ways in which you will permit him to have an influence in how you live — NOW?

He is also our King. That is the third thing that Jesus did and does. When we call Him "King" we are talking about His lordship. People often talk about the lordship of Jesus when they refer to His coming back to earth at the end of time. Then He will set up His eternal kingdom. Those will be grand and glorious times. But if we think of the kingship and lordship of Jesus only in those terms, we will miss out on what it means to have Him as King now, in this time.

What does it mean to have Jesus as the king and lord of your life now?

> Usually when we think of someone as a king, we imagine that person as the one who is served by his subjects. Jesus, however, gave us a new twist to what it means to be king. What is that new twist?
>
> In other words, lordship and leadership now are translated as service, as one who serves. Therefore, be as specific as you can about how you can put the words of Matthew 25 into action. Make definite plans to do at least one of these things within the next 24 hours. How does Ephesians 5:22, "be subject one to another out of reverence for Christ," fit in here?

There are undoubtedly many ways in which that question can be answered. One of the ways which I think is very important is hinted at in the words which Jesus said to His disciples in the very night before He died. He said that He was there with them not as one to be served but as one who serves. Jesus was a king who served others. He made serving a royal, a regal, act.

It was about that same time when He also said this to His disciples:

> *I was hungry and you gave me something to eat.*
> *I was thirsty and you gave me something to drink.*
> *I was without clothing and you clothed me.*
> *I was sick, I was lonely, and you visited me.*
> *I was a stranger and you took me in.*

His disciples said: "Lord, when did we do those sorts of things for you?" Jesus responded:

> *When you do it for others, for the least of your brothers, the homeless, the destitute, the starving, the helpless, when you serve them, then it is like you are serving me.*
> — Matthew 25

There is no better way for us to live the Christian faith, to serve Jesus as Lord, to treat Him as King, to live under his kingship and lordship, than to serve and treat our brothers and sisters as kings and queens.

So there you have it: Jesus as PROPHET, PRIEST, and KING. Now we not only know who Jesus was and is, but we also know what He has done and continues to do for us. Again, however, remember, that the key to all of this is in those little words called "pronouns," those personal pronouns, which remind us that it was for us that Jesus did all of this. Jesus is for us PROPHET, PRIEST, and KING.

Questions

1. What did C.S. Lewis say was "silly" to say about Jesus?

2. What is the work of a prophet?

3. What is the work of a priest?

4. What is the work of a king?

5. What stands at the center of the Christian faith?

6. What chapter in the Bible is known as "The Suffering Servant" chapter?

7. What is one of the finest ways to live the Christian faith?

Discussion

1. Talk about John Updike's Easter witness.

2. Discuss how Jesus is Prophet, Priest, and King in your life.

The Apostles' Creed: Third Article
The Holy Spirit

❖ ❖ ❖ ❖ ❖

Riddle: n. A question or statement requiring thought to answer or understand. Usually a riddle will contain within itself hints to the answer or understanding. Before beginning this chapter answer these three questions: 1) For what do we use our head? 2) For what do we use our hands? 3) And what does it mean when we say that something has no body? Now proceed and answer the riddle: "What has a head and hands but no body?" Remember, the answer is not the only important thing. A proper understanding of each of the three ingredients is also important.

❖ ❖ ❖ ❖ ❖

Question: What has a head and hands but no body?

Answer: The Holy Spirit, or as might be said in older English, "The Holy Ghost."

The question might sound like a strange question. In addition, you might think that the answer is even stranger. Therefore, I would like to explain what I meant by both that question and answer. I'll do so by asking some questions and suggesting some more answers.

First, what is a head for?

For thinking, of course.

And what are hands used for?

For getting things done, of course.

So then, here we have the answers to the first two parts of the question, a riddle of sorts: the Holy Spirit thinks and gets things done.

But we also say that the Holy Spirit has no body. That means, among other things, that the Holy Spirit is invisible.

❖ ❖ ❖ ❖ ❖

There are many things which we know exist but which we can't see. For example, electricity or the wind. But we certainly can see what these invisible forces do. Make a list of a number of these forces and what they do.

❖ ❖ ❖ ❖ ❖

Yes, I must admit that this explanation to the riddle does not give us a complete definition and description of the Holy Spirit, yet it does shed some light on this subject, the subject of the Third Article of the Apostles' Creed: the Holy Spirit.

I believe in the Holy Spirit, the holy Christian church, the communion of saints, the forgiveness of sins, the resurrection of the body, and the life everlasting.

That's saying a lot. What does it all mean? Again, for an answer to those sorts of questions we turn to the explanation of this Third Article as written by Dr. Martin Luther in his well-known *Small Catechism*. Once more he asks the question, "What does this mean?" (What do these words of the Third Article of the Creed mean?) And he gives this answer:

I believe that I cannot by my own reason or strength believe in Jesus Christ, my Lord, or come to Him; but the Holy Spirit has called me by the Gospel, enlightened me with His gifts, sanctified and kept me in the true faith.
In the same way He calls, gathers, enlightens, and sanctifies the whole Christian church on earth, and keeps it with Jesus Christ in the one true faith.
In this Christian church He daily and richly forgives all my sins and the sins of all believers.
On the Last Day He will raise me and all the dead, and give eternal life to me and all believers in Christ.
This is most certainly true.

There is more in those words than what we can possibly talk about at one time. Therefore, I direct your attention primarily to "WHO the Holy Spirit is." I shall talk about the Holy Spirit's "person."

❖ ❖ ❖ ❖ ❖

The word "spirit" is used to designate a lot of things. What are some of the ways in which this word is used? What are some of the things that it identifies?

❖ ❖ ❖ ❖ ❖

We live at a time when people like to have things explained to them. That "explaining" means that they like to have things proven. This is a scientific age, an age of facts and figures. And that makes it rather difficult to speak convincingly of a Spirit, Holy or any other kind, at least if we mean by Spirit something, or someone, that has an identity all of its, his, or her own. I suppose that back in simpler and more primitive times, when people were convinced that their world was inhabited by all sorts of spirits, they found it easier to believe in a Holy Spirit, even if there wasn't much evidence. Those were days when people were convinced that spirits lived in trees or dwelt beneath bridges or flew through the skies on stormy nights.

Today those kinds of spirits are confined and assigned to such make-believe worlds as the movies. Yes, we do hear of satanism and witchcraft which traffic in things "spiritual," but more often than not those who play with those occult curiosities are the kinds of people who demonstrate bizarre and deviant behavior in the first place. Their behavior is usually considered to be either "sick" or criminal. The make-believe world of those people is all twisted out of shape.

❖ ❖ ❖ ❖ ❖

Spirits can be both personal and impersonal. Give examples of each. What is the main difference between a personal and an impersonal spirit?

Personal spirits can be both good and bad. Angels are examples of good spirits. Identify some of the things that angels as good spirits do. Make reference to their appearances in the Bible. For example, Luke 2.

The Bible also has a lot to say about bad (evil) spirits. What is said about them in the following passages?

Genesis 3:1-15	**Matthew 4:1-11**
Leviticus 19:31	**John 8:44**
1 Samuel 28:3-9	**Ephesians 6:11**
2 Kings 23:24	**1 Peter 5:8**

❖ ❖ ❖ ❖ ❖

The mainstream of society, however, likes to have things proven. Here everything must be put into a test tube of sorts so that it can be analyzed. No wonder, then, that it is more difficult for us to accept the idea of a spirit, much less the idea of a Holy Spirit than it was to accept that sort of thing in previous times. Consequently, there is the temptation to dismiss the Holy Spirit as merely some sort of mythological being or fantasy of the imagination. At best we might consider him (or perhaps "it") as something akin to team spirit. A baseball team playing in front of supportive and cheering fans has what is often referred to as a "tenth man" on the team. Team spirit is something like that. It gives you an extra edge. So, "catch the spirit." It's in the air.

Recently in films it was "the Force," a rather nameless and bodiless source of super energy and wisdom, which became another way of speaking about something like the spirit. But then as we all know, those movies were and are only fantasy.

These and other such attempts at describing and defining the Holy Spirit all fall rather short. So let's look again at how Martin Luther addressed this issue. He said:

> *I believe that ... the Holy Spirit has CALLED me ... ENLIGHTENED me ... SANCTIFIED and KEPT me in the true faith ... In the same way He CALLS, GATHERS, ENLIGHTENS, and SANCTIFIES the whole Christian church ... In this church He FORGIVES ... sins.*

Did you notice all those verbs?

❖ ❖ ❖ ❖ ❖

The Holy Spirit is a personal spirit. The Holy Spirit initiates action described by Luther with a number of verbs. List these verbs/words that Luther uses in his explanation to the Third Article. Then give a definition of each of these actions.

❖ ❖ ❖ ❖ ❖

I think that the best way to get to know anything about God (and here the emphasis is on God the Holy Spirit) is by paying attention to what God has done and is doing. God is a God of action. When talking about God the Father, we speak about God who is our creator and who sustains life. When we speak about God the Son, Jesus the Christ, we focus on His act of redeeming us. Now, when we talk about God the Holy Spirit, the third person of the Trinity, we talk about how He calls us into the faith and about how He keeps us there — in the faith.

You see, when speaking about Who the Holy Spirit is, we must speak about What the Holy Spirit does. Therefore, we must ask "And just what is it that He does?"

❖ ❖ ❖ ❖ ❖

Even though the Holy Spirit can not be seen, it is often represented by some sort of symbol. With what kind of symbol would you represent the Holy Spirit? If possible make this symbol. Draw it or demonstrate it.

❖ ❖ ❖ ❖ ❖

As Luther's words of explanation tell us so well, the Holy Spirit calls you and me, He calls us, into the faith. For example, I am not a Christian because I wanted to be one. Oh, yes, I do want to be and remain a Christian. But it was not by my own design that I became one and am one. I am thankful, however, and grateful to my parents who brought me when I was still an infant to the church and saw to it that I was baptized into the family of God. Then, following my baptism, they made sure that during those early years of my life I continued to come to church and attend Sunday school. They put me where that Word of God could get at me, where the Holy Spirit working through that Word of God could get at me and keep me in the faith into which I had been baptized.

❖ ❖ ❖ ❖ ❖
Are you a Christian? How did you become a Christian? What forces (means) were instrumental in making becoming a Christian happen in your life? What role did the Holy Spirit have in all of that?
❖ ❖ ❖ ❖ ❖

The Apostle Paul in his letters to the Ephesians and Timothy, for example, says that without the Word of God working within us, calling us to the faith and actually bringing us into the faith, we would remain dead toward God, "dead in our trespasses and sins." We are very much like stones lying on the ground. We are not going to move all by ourselves. No, we are not going to move unless some force outside of us does the moving. It is the Holy Spirit which provides that moving force for us.

❖ ❖ ❖ ❖ ❖
When something happens *immediately*, it happens directly with no need for a means or an instrument. When something happens *mediately*, some means, some instrument was used. What means are often used by the Holy Spirit to work within our lives?
❖ ❖ ❖ ❖ ❖

We say that the Holy Spirit works and does what He does through the "Means of Grace." The Word of God as we find it in the Bible and the Sacraments of Baptism and Holy Communion are such Means of Grace which the Holy Spirit uses. They are the instruments, the vehicles (Martin Luther sometimes called them the "wagons"), which God uses to bring to us His love, His grace. They are also the instruments, the vehicles, which the Holy Spirit uses to keep in touch with us that we might be kept within the faith.

❖ ❖ ❖ ❖ ❖
The Means of Grace as described by Luther (the Word of God, Baptism, and Holy Communion) are the instruments which the Holy Spirit often uses to work within our lives. How important are each of these Means to you? How do you demonstrate that importance?
❖ ❖ ❖ ❖ ❖

The word "spirit" in the English language means "breath." It is also interesting to note that in the Hebrew and Greek languages (the languages in which the Old and the New Testaments were written) the words for "spirit" (*ruach* and *pneuma*) also mean "breath." Yes, Spirit does mean breath — the breath of God, that eternal life-giving force of God.

The word "spirit" has worked its way into a lot of our words. Make a list containing as many of them as you can. For example: respiration.

It is also important for us to remember that when the Holy Spirit breathes life into common, ordinary words those words become powerful. Yes, then these words become the very Word of God — that same Word of God by which the universe was created. God spoke, and it was so. Then that Word became flesh and dwelt among us. That Word was known as Immanuel, "God is with us." That Word was known as Jesus the Christ.

It is said that the word is the most powerful force on earth. Discuss the power of the word. What can it do? How does it hurt and help people? What have you done with your words lately? How do we make words? How do we say words? From where do our words come? Do you understand now how we breathe life and power and energy into our words? Even though we can't see our words, we certainly can see what our words do!

So it is that the Holy Spirit breathes life into that Word which speaks of Jesus Christ. We call that Word "the Gospel." It is that Gospel which is the power of God even unto salvation.

That Word is also spoken over the waters of Baptism, and they become life-giving waters, eternal life-giving waters, the waters of rebirth. Such waters wash away the terminal illness of sin's consequences.

That Word is also spoken over the bread and the wine of Holy Communion. It is a Word which promises that here is the body and blood of Jesus, "Given and shed for us for the remission of sins." And "whoever believes these words has exactly what they say: forgiveness of sins," and that means life and salvation.

That then is Who the Holy Spirit is. That then is What the Holy Spirit does.

Questions

1. What has a head and hands but no body? Explain.

2. What is the difference between "the Force" and the Holy Spirit?

3. Why is it necessary that the Holy Spirit "call" us to faith?

4. Identify the Means of Grace and what they do.

5. What are some words related to "spirit"?

Discussion

1. Discuss the uniqueness of the Holy Spirit in comparison to such things as team spirit, the Force, and so forth.

2. Discuss the importance of the Means of Grace to the church's ministry.

The Apostles' Creed: Third Article

The Holy Spirit — Comforter And Counselor

❖ ❖ ❖ ❖ ❖
What are some of the things upon which our lives are absolutely dependent (without which we would die)? How important to you is your relationship with God? Is it a matter of life or death?
❖ ❖ ❖ ❖ ❖

"As a tree torn from the soil dies, as a river separated from its source dries up, so the human spirit wanes and grows dim and dull when it is separated from its source of life, God." So wrote a wise man.

In the last chapter we talked about the Holy Spirit calling us into faith in God. Now let's talk about the Holy Spirit keeping us there — in faith in God.

Again, notice the emphasis upon the verbs, those words of action. One of the ways in which we know God, and that includes the Holy Spirit, is by the means of what He has done and by what He continues to do. Those words of action, those verbs which tell us what He has done and continues to do, are so important for us to know.

❖ ❖ ❖ ❖ ❖
Everybody has some fear, fear of things and/or fear of something happening. Perhaps the fear is of spiders or of public speaking or of losing a friend. Make a list of your fears. Rate them on a scale of 1 to 10, 10 representing great fear. For example, fear of spiders might be a 2 while the fear of public speaking might be a 7 or the fear of losing a friend might be a 5.

How do we overcome fears? Are there some fears that might never be overcome? What do we do about them?

❖ ❖ ❖ ❖ ❖

Remember, then, that even as God CALLS us unto the faith, He through the Holy Spirit also KEEPS us there; He keeps us close to Himself. This is how that happens: When Jesus met with His disciples on Maundy Thursday evening in order to celebrate the Passover meal with them, He announced that the next day (which we know as Good Friday) He would have to die on the cross. Of course, His disciples vehemently protested. Have you ever wondered why? Was it because they were really all that concerned about Jesus' welfare, or was it because they now were afraid that they would be without their leader? What was it that they worried about? I think it mostly was that they were afraid that they were going to lose their leader. And I think that was the case, because Jesus picked up on this fear when He said to them:

> *Let not your hearts be troubled ... I will pray the Father, and He will give you another Counselor, to be with you forever, even the Spirit of Truth ... These things I have spoken with you while I am still with you. But the Counselor, the Holy Spirit, whom the Father will send in my name, He will teach you all things, and bring to your remembrance all that I have said to you.* — John 14

How did Jesus provide for his disciples who feared being without Him? Do you find the Holy Spirit to be of much comfort and counsel to you in your frightful moments?

❖ ❖ ❖ ❖ ❖

The Holy Spirit as Counselor, as Comforter, He who will not leave us in the times of our struggles with our faith and for the faith, is the One whom Jesus said would visit us, be near us, and strengthen us.

After His crucifixion and resurrection Jesus met with His disciples on numerous occasions. The last time that He met with them, immediately before He ascended into heaven, He gave them both an assignment and a promise. This is recorded by Matthew as the conclusion to his Gospel. "Go make disciples of all nations, baptizing them in the name of the Father, and of the Son, and of the Holy Spirit ... and I will be with you until the end of time." We call these words "the Great Commission."

In addition to the Great Commission, the Scriptures contain a number of things that God would have us do. Make a list of as many of them as

you can think of, and make a resolve also to do some of them. You will find some of those commissions in the Ten Commandments. Others are found in the Old Testament prophets, and still others in the words of Jesus recorded in the New Testament.

❖ ❖ ❖ ❖ ❖

The question we must now ask is: "But just how would Jesus be with them? Just how will Jesus be with us as He has promised to be?"

Answer: the disciples were instructed to go back to the holy city of Jerusalem; there they were to wait; they were to wait until they would receive "power from on high." That power would be the outpouring of the Holy Spirit who would lead them in all truth.

❖ ❖ ❖ ❖ ❖

The event of Pentecost recorded in Acts 2 was no ordinary event. Read the entire chapter and make a list of some of the out of the ordinary things that happened.

❖ ❖ ❖ ❖ ❖

And that's exactly what happened. Luke, in the first two chapters of his second book in the Bible titled "The Acts of the Apostles," wrote that the disciples did indeed return to Jerusalem. There they waited for ten days. Then it happened. It was the day of Pentecost. Early in the day there descended upon the house where all the disciples were staying a sound like that of a mighty rushing wind. The disciples felt warmed all over. They beamed so much that it seemed as if they were on fire; there was a glow about them. And then they began to speak, to preach, to witness, to proclaim that Jesus was indeed the living, risen, and ascended Lord of all the universe.

The most phenomenal thing about all of this was that the disciples were suddenly speaking this message in all sorts of different languages, languages which they had never studied or spoken before. It was a miracle. It was a miracle of the Holy Spirit.

However, an even greater miracle on that day some 2,000 years ago was that some 3,000 people who heard the disciples speak for Christ were baptized and became members of the church of Christ on earth. What was happening there was that the Holy Spirit was equipping the disciples for their work as apostles. We might say that He was "counseling" them. Perhaps you might say that it was like the Holy Spirit being a coach — even more than just a coach. The Holy Spirit was actually providing the very talents which were required for their carrying out "the Great Commission." We sometimes refer to those talents as "the gifts of the Holy Spirit." They are "spiritual gifts."

❖ ❖ ❖ ❖ ❖
Spiritual gifts are special blessings that the Holy Spirit gives to "disciples" so that they can fulfill what they have been commissioned to do. Romans 12:6-8, 1 Corinthians 12:4-11, Ephesians 4:11-12, and 1 Peter 4:10-11 contain partial lists of spiritual gifts. Identify as many as you can from these lists, and then describe how they can be used in the church today.
❖ ❖ ❖ ❖ ❖

That's what Saint Paul calls them in the first letter which he wrote to the Christian congregation at Corinth:

> *Now concerning spiritual gifts ... to each is given the manifestation of the Spirit for the common good. To one is given through the Spirit the utterance of wisdom, and to another the utterance of knowledge according to the same Spirit ... All these are inspired by one and the same Spirit.* — 1 Corinthians 12

Paul lists more gifts of the Holy Spirit in Romans 12 and in Ephesians 4. Still more can be found in 1 Peter 4.

These gifts are given "for the common good," Paul says. The Spirit counsels and comforts; He inspires; He ministers to those of the faith so that they can in turn minister to others. That's the way Jesus has provided for His church and for those of His church in the "in between time," in between the time He ascended into heaven and the time when He will return in glory. It is the Holy Spirit who makes things happen. Read the Book of Acts of the Apostles. It is a "spirit filled" book. It records many accounts of the Apostles, filled with the Spirit, sensitive to His presence and power, making things happen. Over and over again we are told that many were baptized, that they were added to the church, and that miracles even took place. There were many such wonders. It is impossible to miss. When the Spirit was present with the disciples, things happened.

Acts is a "spirit-filled" book. Read the entire Book of Acts and note the many references to the Holy Spirit being at work. Note the verbs that are used to describe the Holy Spirit's activity.

The Holy Spirit works in both dramatic and in quiet ways. Frequently the Holy Spirit addresses us in moments of quiet meditation. Try meditation for half an hour. Do not worry about filling the time with things to say. Rather, open yourself to the speaking of the Holy Spirit. It is suggested that your time of meditation have a focus and a theme. Perhaps that would be some difficulty or struggle that you are encountering. Or perhaps it is a concern for someone else whom you know. Then let the Holy Spirit go to work. You might want to begin and end your time of meditation with the words of this hymn verse:

Breathe on me, breath of God,
Fill me with life anew,
That I may love all that you love
And do what you would do.

❖ ❖ ❖ ❖ ❖

Sometimes however, the presence of the Spirit is encountered in less dramatic ways. These encounters are important, too. Let me explain, using an example from the Old Testament, from 1 Kings 19. This is a chapter from the story about Elijah, a prophet of God. Elijah had become very disappointed. He was on the verge of losing his faith because of the lack of success he had encountered while being a faithful servant of God. Therefore, he went out into the wilderness. He wanted to die. But God prodded him along until he came to that very holy mountain called Sinai. There God had a revelation for him. As Elijah stood upon the mountain, he witnessed first the rush of a mighty wind. Elijah was expecting God to talk to him, but the voice of God did not sound in the strong wind this time. Then we are told that Elijah witnessed an earthquake. Still no voice of God. The earthquake was followed by a spectacular fire. Again no voice from God even though Elijah was standing on the very mountain on which Moses stood when God talked to him. Finally, however, God did speak, but He spoke to Elijah in a "still, small voice." There was encouragement in that still, small voice. God was counseling and comforting Elijah.

The point of this is that we too sometimes must seek the voice of the Spirit of God not in that which is spectacular but in the "stillness of the night," if you will.

We are a people who like the showy, the spectacular. However, God often works in very modest ways. That's why while there is a time to speak, there is also a time to keep silent. There is a time to be silent under the Word of God so that it can speak to us. That's what the Psalmist meant when he said, "Commune with your heart and be still" (Psalm 4:4). That is the simple silence of you and me realizing that at that particular moment what God has to say to us just might be more important than what we think we must say to Him, or to anyone else for that matter. After all, He already knows our every thought. This is that kind of silence which a child knows when his father walks into the room. He is about to listen to what his father has to say.

Some people call that meditation, that special exercise of time when the Holy Spirit communes with us. That's not empty time, or even a time for empty-minded wanderings. No. That is a time for a quiet turning into the Word, the Scriptures, and focusing on them and what they have to say to us. As God breathes into them and through them, He breathes His Spirit into our lives.

Such is the work of the Holy Spirit as He breathes into us the very breath of God, the very wisdom and counsel of God which brings us into the faith and which keeps us in the faith so that we can be about our Father's business, which is doing what His Son and our Brother, Jesus, has asked us as His disciples to do.

Questions

1. How would Jesus be present with His disciples after His ascension?

2. Where in the Bible can you find the mention of spiritual gifts?

Discussion

1. Review the incidents of the first Pentecost (Acts 2).

2. Discuss ways in which the Holy Spirit "comforts and counsels" to this day.

3. Compare the more spectacular manifestations of the Holy Spirit to the less dramatic ways in which the Spirit demonstrates its power.

The Apostles' Creed: Third Article
The Church

Name as many church denominations as you can. Now identify as many church congregations in your town or area as you can. Which of these churches do you think is/are best? What makes a church "good" in your eyes? How would you rate your church? Is it "good"? If so, what makes it good?

Why do you think that there are so many different church denominations? Why do you think that there are so many different congregations in your town or area?

There are a lot of churches from which to choose these days: Lutheran churches, Baptist churches, Presbyterian churches, Roman Catholic churches, independent churches; Saint Luke, Saint John, Saint Mary. Which is the true church? Which is the right one? Would you like to know? Let me tell you.

I would not be surprised if you are thinking that since I am a Lutheran pastor that I am going to say that the answer to the question, "Which is the true church?" is "Why, of course, the Lutheran church."

Lutherans sometimes tell the story about a Methodist who died and went to heaven. As he was being given a guided tour of the place by Saint Peter, he asked as they were walking down the road passing a high stone fence, "By the way, Saint Peter, what's behind that fence?" The Keeper of the Keys answered, "Shhhhh. The Lutherans are over there; don't let them hear you; they think they are the only ones here."

Well, Lutherans don't have a corner on the heaven market. They will not be the only ones there. Nevertheless, the questions still remain: "Today, which is the true church? Where can it be found?" There are so many churches, you know. There are literally hundreds of different denominations. There are numerous varieties of worship styles. And, yes, there are even many kinds of doctrines and teachings. If you take a close look, it will be quite obvious to you that these churches do not all say the same thing. It is not too difficult to conclude that if there is a right church, all of them do not qualify for the honor.

There are many styles of worship. Identify and describe some of them. What are the strong and the weak points of these various styles of worship? Some people think that styles of worship are not much different than styles of clothing or cars or houses. What do you think about that?

Marshall McLuhan, a communication theorist, once said that "How you say something is as important as what you say." What do you think about that? Is there a relationship between style and content in what we say and in how we worship?

Do you think that when it comes to the "true" or "right" church something more is involved than just style?

The Third Article of the Apostles' Creed says, "I believe in the Holy Spirit, the holy Christian church," that is, the true church. But where is it? Where can it be found? How can it be identified?

Some rather significant clues for the answer to these questions can be found in the Scriptures themselves. For example, in Matthew 28 (at the very end of Matthew's last chapter) we read what is most often referred to as "the Great Commission." In His farewell to His disciples, Jesus said:

> *Go therefore and make disciples of all nations, baptizing them in the name of the Father and of the Son and of the Holy Spirit, teaching them to observe all that I have commanded you; and lo, I am with you always to the close of the age.*

Earlier in his Gospel Matthew records Jesus saying, "Wherever two or three are gathered in my name, there I am in the midst of them."

Some people object to the institutionalizing of the church, the organization of the church. What do you think are some of the strengths and some of the weaknesses of the institutional church?

I think, therefore, that it is safe to say that the real church, the true church, is wherever those who believe in Jesus as the Savior gather together in order to do what He has told them to do. And what has He told them to do? Answer: To make disciples. And how are disciples made? Answer: By sharing with others the good news of God's love through Jesus Christ.

In the Lutheran church we like to say that the church is wherever the gospel is preached and people are baptized. However, remember that the church is not so much a place as it is a people, a people who are doing what Jesus has commissioned them to do.

Verbs can describe as well as nouns. Make a list of nouns which identify the church (for example, a building or a congregation). Now follow each of these nouns with verbs which describe the action that belongs to each. You should end up with a list of words which describe what churches do. Assign a value between 1 and 10 (10 being the best) to each of the actions.

When we were talking about the First Article of the Apostles' Creed, I asked the question, "Who is God?" At that time I said that the best way to describe who God is, is to talk about what He has done. At that time I said that God was like a verb. God is known by us for His action. He is known by us for what He does. And I think that the same thing can and should be said about God's people, the church.

Another way of saying this is that the church is where and when the Word of God gets out, where the Gospel is heard, where and when people come to faith in Jesus because of this Gospel which comes through the spoken word, and which comes to us through the sacraments of Holy Baptism and Holy Communion which are empowered by the Word. The church is wherever and whenever the Gospel is in action, and through this action the Holy Spirit works faith in the hearts and lives of people, so that men, women, and children (people of all nations) might come to believe in Jesus as the Christ, the One who is the Savior of all nations.

Oh, yes, the church does other things, too, which are also important. For example, the church sponsors and supports programs of caring for folks who may be "down and out." The church (church people, Gospel people) visits the sick and supports and promotes moral causes. They foster fellowship. They engage in programs of education. Nevertheless, we must always remember that the most important task of the church, the characteristic which signals where the church really is and when it really is, is where and when people give witness to the Gospel. That is the most important mark of the true church.

In the Third Article of the Apostles' Creed we also confess, "I believe in ... the communion of saints." Now, what do you suppose that means? Sometimes we might think that the words "communion of saints" refer to the Sacrament of Holy Communion, the Sacrament of the Altar, the Eucharist. Well, yes, we do believe in Holy Communion as one of the means whereby God gets through to us, but in this part of the Creed the words "communion of saints" refer to the fellowship of believers.

Let's take a look at that phrase, "the communion of saints." First, what do we mean by the word "communion"? It is very similar in meaning to "fellowship" (used as a noun, not as a verb). The church is a fellowship of people who need each other — who need each other to speak to each other of the love and of the forgiveness and of the grace of God, reminding each other that God indeed is a loving Father, a Father of prodigals, which we all are.

There are many reasons given by various persons for not belonging to a church, a congregation. Make a list of some of them. What do you think of these reasons? Are they good ones? Do you ever feel like using one or some of them?

That reminds me of a protest which we sometimes hear. Some people say, "Just being a member of a congregation does not make a person a Christian." True, but then on the other hand, not being a member of a congregation and still being a Christian, being a "lone wolf" Christian, is about as exciting as a one-man parade, or as risky as a one-man baseball team. They are rather unimpressive and inefficient. To put it another way, fingers no longer attached to the hand soon decay, and little children left by themselves soon die. The simple fact is that if Christians are going to be healthy, and if they are going to get much done as Christians, they need each other. There simply is no substitute for that.

There are many things in life for which we need the assistance of other people. Some of these things are important and some not so important. What are some things that you can do without the help of others? What are some of the things which you cannot do without the help of others?

Paul in 1 Corinthians refers to "the communion of saints" as the "body of Christ." He writes, "For just as the body is one and has many members and all the members of the body, though many are one body, so it is with Christ ... You are the body of Christ, and individually members of it."

❖ ❖ ❖ ❖ ❖
Symbiosis: n. The relationship of two or more different organisms in a close association that "may be ... of benefit to each." The word "symbiosis" is made up of two Greek words: *sym/n* which means "with" and *bios* which means "life." Therefore symbiosis means "to live with." Name a few symbiotic relationships. In what ways can members of a church (congregation) be in a symbiotic relationship with each other? (What are some other words in the English language which employ *sym/n* and *bios*? Hint: symphony and biology.)
❖ ❖ ❖ ❖ ❖

That is good! Oh, sometimes we might complain about it or protest about it, but it is good that we have the opportunity to be members of the communion of saints, a Christian fellowship, a congregation. In spite of all the differences of opinion we sometimes may have, and in spite of the fact that we sometimes have a hard time getting along with each other, having each other is better than not having each other.

❖ ❖ ❖ ❖ ❖
When speaking of a "saint" we usually mean someone whose behavior is exceptionally good. What are some examples of saintly behavior?
❖ ❖ ❖ ❖ ❖

Don't forget to thank God for one another.

Now let's take a look at the second word in the phrase "communion of saints": saints. Show me one! Show me just one church where all the members, the entire communion, are saint-like, where all the members live holy lives, lives above reproach. The truth of the matter is that most churches, congregations, seem to be made up of a lot of hypocrites. Haven't you heard people say:

I wouldn't ever go to that church. No, sir! I wouldn't be caught dead there. There are too many hypocrites there. You ought to see how they behave on a Saturday night, and then they go to church on Sunday morning and think that everything is all right again.

❖ ❖ ❖ ❖ ❖
A "hypocrite" usually refers to a person who says one thing (good) but does another (bad). (This is another word that comes from the Greek language. It refers to a person who only "plays" a part. We might call that kind of person a "phoney.") Describe some of the hypocrites you have known in your life. Identify them. What are some of the hypocritical behaviors that really irritate you? Do you ever engage in those kinds of behavior?
❖ ❖ ❖ ❖ ❖

I suppose that there are a lot of hypocrites in church. I tell the members of my confirmation classes that the more sinners and hypocrites we have in church the better. Church is not for people who have never done anything wrong. It is not for perfect people. No! It is for imperfect people. The church is exactly where sinners, all types and kinds (including hypocrites), should and need to be. For that is where the Word has the best chance to get at them.

❖ ❖ ❖ ❖ ❖

Do you agree or disagree with the proposition that church is the right place for hypocrites? Think through your answer and give as much supporting material, as many reasons as you can, in defense of your answer.

❖ ❖ ❖ ❖ ❖

In other words, church is where sinners belong. The more sinners in church the better. Jesus Himself said, "The whole (the healthy) do not need a physician. But those who are ill do." The "holy Joes" of this world don't need a Savior (at least they don't think that they do). But I do! And I know a lot of other sinners who do. Quite frankly, I enjoy seeing them in church on Sunday morning, even if I might be a bit uncomfortable with what they did on Saturday night. Being at church is being at one of the best places where they can take care of what went wrong the night before. There (here) they (we) hear the Word of the Gospel, the word of forgiveness, spoken, and we become God's saints, His communion of saints, not because of something which we have done, but because of what He has done for us through our Savior, Jesus. Now when God looks at us as we stand together under the cross He sees saints.

And that is what the church is; that is what we are — a fellowship of disciples who in addition to caring for the people of the world have nothing finer to do than to share the Gospel of Christ with the world.

Questions

1. What is the nature of the Great Commission? (Matthew 28)

2. What are some of the other legitimate functions of the church?

3. What do we mean by "the communion of saints"?

4. Where do hypocrites belong? Why?

Discussion

1. There are many churches (denominations) in the world today. Discuss which are part of the "true" church.

2. Does your church have a clear focus on what it is supposed to be and do? Help to sharpen that focus.

3. Discuss "the Body of Christ" (1 Corinthians 12) and compare it with being a "lone wolf" Christian. What implications does that have for the local congregation?

The Apostles' Creed: Third Article

The Forgiveness Of Sins ...

Resurrection ... Life Everlasting

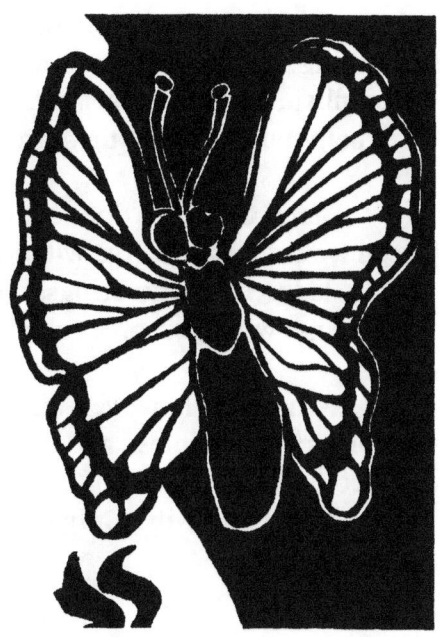

❖ ❖ ❖ ❖ ❖

There seems to be a logical progression from "the forgiveness of sins" to "the resurrection" to "life everlasting." Think about it. Why does one lead to the other?

❖ ❖ ❖ ❖ ❖

I believe in the Holy Spirit ... the forgiveness of sins, the resurrection of the body, and the life everlasting.

With these words we come to the end of our discussion of not only the Third Article of the Apostles' Creed but also the end of the entire Apostles' Creed itself. These three concluding items, the forgiveness of sins, the resurrection of the body, and life everlasting, fit well together, for where there is the forgiveness of sins, you can count on the resurrection of the body, and there certainly will also be life everlasting — life with God forever.

❖ ❖ ❖ ❖ ❖

What is your definition of "being alive," of "life"? What are some of the things that "living things" do? Why, then, do you think most of us fear being dead? Do you see the connection between being dead (physically) and being "dead in trespasses and sins"?

❖ ❖ ❖ ❖ ❖

Consider this: Being unforgiven is as good as being dead. That is what Saint Paul meant when he wrote about the unforgiven person "being dead in trespasses and sins" (Ephesians 2:1). Being dead in sin means that the unforgiven sins are like a dead weight hanging around a person's neck, pulling him down and down and down. If that person is ever going to lift up his head again, something needs to be done about that dreadful weight. The doing of that, however, cannot be accomplished by the person already dead. Dead people do not initiate any action or activity. Therefore, help must come to them from the outside, from outside of the person.

Thank God help does come. Thank God that life-giving help does come. That is why in the Creed we confess and give witness that by the grace of God, the Holy Spirit, the Third Person of the Trinity, is the One who brings to us new life through the forgiveness of sins. Yes, it is the forgiveness of sins which becomes a new life-giving power within us now and which lasts even forever.

Remember, however, that this life-giving power must come from somewhere, and since the dead are rather helpless and unable to initiate or accomplish anything by themselves, this power must come from outside of them. Dead people do not spontaneously generate life, or for that matter, any kind of activity. Only in make-believe horror movies do the dead do anything, and we know that is not for real.

There are some things in this world which do "spontaneously generate" some sort of activity. Consider gasoline-soaked rags that are confined to a small, unvented, and hot area. They will explode. That is an action. How does that kind of action differ from action initiated by human beings? How is action initiated by God (the Holy Spirit) different from human action?

The real truth is that our sins have signed and sealed our death warrant. We are by nature dead toward God. That is very real. And if there is going to be any chance at new life, the power for the life must come from outside of us. Yes, it must come from Him who is the very Author of life; it must come from God.

The wonderful thing is that even though by nature we all are dead in our trespasses and sins (the reality of our condition by birth), new life toward, with, and in God is something we can all experience now, in this time, in this life as a sign of greater things still to come in the resurrected life. And that is also for real.

No wonder then that we confess in the Third Article of the Apostles' Creed that by no stretch of anyone's imagination is this resurrected life merely an idea of fantasy. Instead, when Christians confess that they believe in the resurrection of the dead, that is exactly what they mean: a real, live resurrection, not just a fanciful wish for the future or some symbolic new lease on life in this present life. Let me put it this way: We physical/spiritual people who know what it is like to die will also experience a real resurrection. The Bible calls it a "bodily resurrection." In eternity, we will not just be spirits floating around in the sky somewhere, sitting down every now and then on the corner of some cloud in order to play our golden harps.

❖ ❖ ❖ ❖ ❖
Concern about the resurrection has affected many people's feeling about funerals and what to do with a body once it is dead. What do you think about the disposition of the body? Is cremation all right? How comfortable are you with donating body organs for transplants or for research? How about the business of autopsies? Make sure you back up your answers with more than just "feelings." Have some good reasons.
❖ ❖ ❖ ❖ ❖

One of the finest expressions of the reality of both death and resurrection comes from the contemporary author, John Updike. Specifically, speaking of the reality of the death and the resurrection of Jesus, he writes:

> *Make no mistake; if He rose at all*
> *it was as His body;*
> *if the cells' dissolution did not reverse, the molecules reknit,*
> *   the amino acids rekindle*
> *the Church will fall.*
>
> *It was not as the flowers,*
> *each soft spring recurrent;*
> *it was not as His Spirit in the mouths and fuddled eyes of the*
> *   eleven apostles;*
> *it was as His flesh: ours.*
>
> *The same hinged thumbs and toes,*
> *the same valved heart*
> *that — pierced — died, withered, paused and then regathered*
> *   out of His father's might,*
> *new strength to enclose.*
>
> *Let us not mock God with metaphor,*
> *analogy, sidestepping transcendence,*
> *making of the event a parable, a sign painted in the faded*
> *   credulity of earlier ages:*
> *let us walk through the door.*
>
> *The stone is rolled back, not papier-mâché,*
> *not a stone in a story,*
> *but the vast rock of materiality that in the slow grinding of*
> *   time will eclipse for each of us*
> *the wide light of day.*
>
> *And if we will have an angel at the tomb,*
> *make it a real angel,*
> *weighty with Max Planck's quanta, vivid with hair, opaque in*
> *   the dawn light, robed in real linen*
> *spun on a definite loom.*

> *Let us not seek to make it less monstrous,*
> *for our own convenience, our own sense of beauty,*
> *lest, awakened in one unthinkable hour, we are embarrassed*
> > *by the miracle,*
> *and crushed by remonstrance.*
> — "Seven Stanzas at Easter" by John Updike

Updike is telling us that if there is a resurrection at all it has to be a real one, not just one of the mind, but real in the terms of the created stuff of this world. You see, the Christian faith is not just a faith of ideas; it is not just philosophy. Instead, it is a faith which revolves around a real and created world and around an act of salvation which was made of flesh and blood. God did not just love us at a distance, blowing us a kiss from heaven every now and then. No! In Jesus He put His arms around our bodies; He embraced us; He bled for us; He even died for us; so He was also resurrected — for real! After His resurrection He even ate fish with His disciples, and we know that ghosts, phantoms, and airy spirits don't eat fish or anything else for that matter.

There seems to have always been a lot of dreaming about what life after death will be like. While the Bible rules out the possibility of reincarnation (coming back to life again in another form of life; Hebrews 9:27), much has been said and written about the hereafter. You might, for example, want to consult Dante's book *The Inferno*. It speaks about eternal life in hell. The Book of Revelation has a number of interesting things to say about life in heaven (Revelation 7, 14, 21, 22). What do you think (wish) heaven will be like? Can we be sure of the details?

The point in all of this is that even as Christ physically, bodily, was resurrected, so will we be. That's what we believe, teach, and confess through the words of the Third Article of this ancient and ecumenical Creed.

What I have just said (and, obviously, others have said it, too) has given rise to many questions about what this resurrected life will be like. Those kinds of questions have been around ever since Christ was resurrected from the grave. Paul in his well-known fifteenth chapter of 1 Corinthians included some examples of these questions which had been asked of him by converts to the Christian faith.

"How are the dead raised?"

"What kind of bodies will they have in heaven?"

"What will we look like?"

I like the way that Paul handled those questions. Please don't take offense, but he simply responded by saying, "You foolish man (people)." He meant: "Why are you bothering your heads with such questions? Why do you waste your time in such idle speculation? All that we need to know now is that there will be a resurrection. It will be a resurrection. It will be for real!

❖ ❖ ❖ ❖ ❖

All of us have probably attended a funeral at some time or other: the funeral of a family member, or of a friend, or a neighbor. All of us will be part of a funeral some day, our own. What do you think is the purpose of a funeral? How would you like your funeral to go? What about visitation at a funeral home? How about flowers or memorial gifts? Try your hand at constructing a funeral service: choose hymns, or scripture readings, or other ingredients which you think would be both important and meaningful.

❖ ❖ ❖ ❖ ❖

However, even as it is difficult to compare apples and oranges, so it will be difficult to compare and define the resurrection and life forever with the lives that we live now.

Lo, I tell you a mystery [Saint Paul says]. *We will all be changed, in a moment, in the twinkling of an eye ... And we will be raised, and our perishable nature will put on the imperishable, mortality will put on immortality.* — 1 Corinthians 15

Benjamin Franklin, one of the fathers of our country, caught this spirit very well (as perhaps only he could have caught it). He gave expression to the resurrection through this epitaph which appears on his tombstone to this day:

The body of Benjamin Franklin, printer
Like the cover of an old book, its contents
torn out and stripped of its lettering and gilding
lies here, food for worms.
But the work will not be lost,
For it will appear once more
In a new and more elegant edition,
Revised and corrected by the Author.

I suppose that we too could idly speculate on what the resurrection life will be like. And I imagine that we do. But I am afraid that such idle speculation is not worth much more than wondering and worrying about what is the condition of people between the time of death and the resurrection. We always want answers to those kinds of questions. We want to nail those kinds of things down. Maybe that is because of our insecurities, our doubts, our little faith. Perhaps we just don't trust God enough that He will take care of all those things.

In the face of all of that the Third Article of the Apostles' Creed reminds us one last time that we must turn it all over to God. He was responsible for creating us in the first place. And He must be the One responsible for re-creating us in the second place. Confessing, then, these words of the Third Article of the Creed reminds us that in faith we turn over our destinies to God. He is the Author and the Finisher of our lives. In Him we live, move, and have our very being now and forever.

If you have grieved or are grieving over the death of someone important and close to you, what would you like to have said to you? How would you like other people to treat you? If you know someone who has lost someone close to them, what would you say to that person? How would you treat them?

Questions

1. From where must come help for a dead person?

2. What does it mean to be "dead toward God"?

3. Why is confessing the Third Article of the Apostles' Creed an act of faith?

Discussion

1. Discuss the nature of the "bodily" resurrection.

2. Share what you know about what the Day of Resurrection will be like.

The Lord's Prayer

The Lord's Prayer
The Introduction To
The Lord's Prayer

❖ ❖ ❖ ❖ ❖

What is your prayer life like? How often do you pray? When do you pray? How long do you pray? Do you use memorized prayers or make up your own prayers, or do you use a combination of each? For what do you pray? Are you satisfied with your prayer life? How could you improve it? What are some of the things which interfere with your prayer life? Are you embarrassed to pray in public? If you were asked to lead a group in prayer, what would you do? How would you do it? How do you feel about people who are at ease in leading prayer in public?

❖ ❖ ❖ ❖ ❖

Our Father who art in heaven.

What does this mean? With these words God tenderly invites us to believe that He is our true Father and that we are His true children, so that with all boldness and confidence we may ask Him as dear children ask their dear father.

Once upon a time there was a little Alpine village tucked away among the mountains quite a distance from the main road. It was a self-sufficient little community. It had all the necessary craftsmen and people of different talents to provide its citizens with everything that they needed. There was the butcher and the baker, the carpenter and the miller, the teacher and the preacher, and so forth. But one day the clockmaker died. He was not terribly missed at first. After all, he had been a rather quiet man. However, in the course of time many of the clocks of that little village became annoyingly inaccurate, so much so that a good number of the citizens just let their clocks run down until they stopped keeping time. They made no attempt to rewind them. After all, the clocks were no longer keeping accurate time, and nobody knew how to do anything about it. Nevertheless, there were some folks who felt that as long as the clocks were running they should be rewound every day no matter how inaccurate they had become. And that is exactly what they did.

One day news spread through the town that a new clockmaker had arrived. Everybody rushed to him with their clocks. But the only ones that he could repair were those that had been kept running. The clocks that had been abandoned had become too rusty.

That little story is about prayer. It points out a very important aspect of prayer: One must do it even if it is not done well, or one will soon forget how to do it altogether.

❖ ❖ ❖ ❖ ❖
List as many kinds of prayer and as many times for prayer as you can think of.
❖ ❖ ❖ ❖ ❖

What is prayer?

Some might say, "Prayer is talking with God."

Or, "Prayer is asking God for things."

Or, better yet, "Prayer is telling God things, especially thanking God for things."

The truth is that prayer is all of these things.

There also are many kinds and types of prayer.

We pray in church.

We pray before and after meals.

Some say their prayers in the morning, some at night, and some say them at both times and at more times.

Many would say, "Prayer should come from the heart."

Others say, "One should pray when in the Spirit," that is, under the influence of the Spirit of God.

There are those who say, "Prayer should contain the best language we can speak." Therefore, prayer should be carefully worked out; prayers should not be random, extemporaneous bursts of words.

❖ ❖ ❖ ❖ ❖
Some people say that prayer should consist of the best language we can muster; others think that prayer should use language which is genuine and which comes from the heart regardless of how poetic it might or might not be. What do you think?

What does it mean to "pray in the Spirit"? Does that mean that we pray in a state of ecstasy or that we permit the Holy Spirit to give direction to our conversation with God?
❖ ❖ ❖ ❖ ❖

There is a bit of truth in all of that. All of that is what prayer is. Now I would like to ask you, "But why pray?"

I think that a good answer to that question is: Because our Father, our Father in heaven, wants to hear from us. Look at it this way: I am a father. I have children. They are sometimes very happy, and they are sometimes very sad. I think that I can tell which time is which without even asking them what it is that has either made them happy or sad. Fathers usually are able to figure those sorts of things out. But even if I am "in the know," I usually ask them, "Why are you so sad?" or "What has made you so happy?" I ask them because I want them to talk to/with me. I want them to tell me, on their own, what is going on even if I already know. And do you know something? Even though they might not know it, they really want to tell me. They feel good if they have someone to talk to about what is going on in their lives. And if they don't practice that kind of talking, they might end up by not talking to anyone at all.

❖ ❖ ❖ ❖ ❖
The "silent treatment" is when someone refuses to talk to someone else. Why does the "silent treatment" hurt so much? Has anyone ever given you that treatment? Have you ever treated someone that way? The "silent treatment" can be especially devastating within the family. Why is that so?

Have you ever wanted to talk to someone even though you already know what he or she is going to say, or even if that person already knows what you are going to say? Why is that conversation still important?
❖ ❖ ❖ ❖ ❖

So also, whatever the circumstances might be, our heavenly Father wants to hear from us, even if He already knows what is on our minds — which, of course, He does know. Nevertheless, He wants us to talk with Him about those sorts of things, or we too might find it hard talking to Him at all anymore.

Therefore, the Lord's Prayer begins with the words, "Our Father" (Abba Father; Dear Father).

What does this mean? With these words God tenderly invites us to believe that He is our true Father and that we are His true children, so that with all boldness and confidence we may ask Him as dear children ask their dear father.

There are two things here that we should note very well: 1) God invites us to pray, and 2) He promises to hear us.

As an earthly father I might not always want to be pestered by what my children have to say. Yes, I must admit, that there are times when I would just as soon that they leave me alone. But this is not so with our heavenly Father. There are no times when He is too busy or too tired. "Behold, He that keeps Israel neither slumbers or sleeps" (Psalm 121). There is no time which is an inconvenience to Him.

One of the big problems we have with talking to each other is that often times one person or the other is too busy to be bothered. What message do you get when someone is too busy to listen to you? What message do you send when you are too busy? Do you think that God is ever too busy?

Therefore, we have the invitation: "Pray without ceasing" (1 Thessalonians 5:17). That does not mean we are to participate in incessant jabbering. God does not hear us because of our many words. But whenever we have something to say to Him, then it is time to talk.

Therefore, we see that the introduction to the Lord's Prayer, "Our Father who art in heaven," is first of all an invitation, an invitation which is to be accepted by children of the heavenly Father. It is our privilege to talk with Him.

The second point in Luther's explanation to the Lord's Prayer is that he tells us that we should pray with "all boldness and confidence." We should, we can, do that because we have the promise that God will hear. Praying like that means that we pray with trust. It is NOT prayer bringing a request before God saying, "You probably won't give me what I'm asking for, but it won't hurt to ask." That is an insult. That is an insult to God.

Why do you think that it is an insult to pray to God while expecting Him either not to hear or not to answer? Do you think that we can make demands of God in our prayers? Are there times when you have lost patience with God because what you asked for was right and decent

> and He just didn't give it to you? (For example, you prayed for someone's health, or for some project at church, or for the stilling of a storm.)

Nevertheless, experience teaches us that we don't always get that for which we ask. That can be very frustrating. It can even make us want to give up on praying at all. In such frustrating moments the Germans sometimes say, *"Ich kann nicht mehr beten."* (I just can't pray anymore.)

My parents told me that the reason we don't always get everything for which we ask is because God knows what is best for us. Therefore, just like a wise father will not give his three-year-old son a loaded gun, so God, knowing that often times we are a lot like three-year-olds, does not give us all the things for which we ask. He knows better. He knows what is best for us.

There might be some truth to that. However, I have a hard time seeing how a sunny sky after a week of rain would really be all that harmful to me and my neighbors. Quite frankly, I think that it would be an improvement. But then, again, thinking that prayer is primarily an exercise in asking for things, even for sunny skies, misses the point.

> What is the connection between the Lord's Prayer and Matthew 6:33? Therefore, what is the primary prayer of the people of God? How hard is it for you to put the welfare of the Kingdom of God ahead of your own welfare? Is it possible to do that? Why do you think it is necessary to pray the Lord's Prayer so often? (What can be the danger of praying it "too" often? Do you think that it can be prayed "too" often?)

Jesus' disciples approached Him and asked: "Lord, teach us to pray." By that they meant: "Lord, teach us to pray right." It was not that they did not know how to pray. I am sure that each of them learned their prayers well as children. They, even as we do, learned their prayers for mealtimes, for bedtimes, prayers for worship, and so forth. Well then, what do you suppose they meant when they asked, "Lord, teach us to pray"?

I think that in their prayers they were after something more than just what they could get. They knew that prayer was more than just asking for things: "Gimme this, gimme that." (If that is all we think that prayer is for, then we might very well pass for being "Gimme Pigs." Selfish. Interested only in getting what we want.)

Yes, the disciples were after something more than that. "Lord, teach us to pray as the Father would have us pray."

But just what does the Father want to hear from us?

What He wants from us is the "Lord's" Prayer not "our" prayer. What I mean by that is that in the Lord's Prayer we get beyond our own private wants and selfish preoccupations. In the Lord's Prayer we are seeking the welfare of the Kingdom of God and then all other things will be given to us as well (Matthew 6).

That's it! The Lord's Prayer is the prayer of the disciples, those who have the responsibility of promoting the welfare of the Kingdom of God among humankind until the Son of Man returns. That then is the concern of the "Our Father." That is how we should pray.

When we pray like that Jesus promises, "Whatever you ask the Father in my name, He will give it to you" (John 14). When He made that promise Jesus was not talking about pennies from heaven; He wasn't even talking about sunny skies. He was talking about the Father answering the petitions of the Kingdom prayer, the family prayer of the children of the heavenly Father. Yes, the Lord's Prayer is our family prayer, the prayer of God's family. It is His children saying, "Abba Father, dear Father, we have something we'd like to discuss with you." That's how Jesus has taught us to pray.

At the beginning of this chapter you were asked to explain what "praying in the Spirit" was. After reading these next few paragraphs again, answer the question: What is praying in the Spirit?

That is also praying under the Spirit of God. To pray under the influence of the Spirit of God does not mean that such praying is done in some sort of trance, but to pray like that is to pray so moved by the Spirit of God that we seek the welfare of the Kingdom as opposed to being moved by the spirit of our own selfish interests.

Thus we pray, "Abba, Father, we need your help in being your people; so send us your Spirit, so that we seek the good of your family." And that is what the seven petitions of the Lord's Prayer are all about. We'll look at them one by one. Meanwhile, keep that clock wound, even if you feel as if you don't know all that you should know about how to pray properly and well. Keep the clock wound. Keep on talking with God. The more you do it, the better at it you will become.

The number 7 is the number which represents that which is holy and that which is complete. It is the number which represents heaven. It is the number which represents the Kingdom of God. Therefore, it is appropriate that the Lord's Prayer, the prayer of God's Kingdom, has seven petitions.

Questions

1. Why could so many of the clocks in the Alpine village not be repaired?

2. Why does God want us to pray even though He knows what our prayers will be?

3. How much should we pray?

4. What does it mean to pray in the Spirit?

Discussion

1. Share with others details about your prayer life.

2. Discuss ways in which your congregation can help people improve their prayer lives.

The Lord's Prayer
The First Petition

❖ ❖ ❖ ❖ ❖
Many people feel as if their religion and religious lives are personal/private affairs and nobody's business but their own. Do you agree with that opinion? In what ways is religion a personal/private affair? What might be the limits of such a view? When is religion a community or family event and something to be shared? How important is this side of religion?
❖ ❖ ❖ ❖ ❖

"Our Father who art in heaven." We don't pray "My Father," nor do we pray "Your Father," but we pray "Our Father." I have always thought it interesting that nowhere in this prayer of prayers do we find the first person singular pronoun employed. Nowhere do we find the words, "My Father who art in heaven … give me this day my daily bread," and so forth. I think that the reason for that is that this grandest of all prayers is not my private prayer, nor is it your private prayer. Instead, it is "our" prayer; it is the prayer of the family, of God's family, the church. Therefore, together we pray. This is a family affair. Faith in the Abba Father, our dear heavenly Father, trusting Him enough to talk with Him about family business, is always a family affair. We don't do it alone, by ourselves. We do it together. Therefore, let us also together now look at each of the seven petitions of this prayer of the family of God.

The first petition, or the first of the seven prayers included in this one prayer, is: "Our Father, who art in heaven, hallowed be Thy name." That means "Holy be Your name." As we can see, the subject of the First Petition is the name of God. That is an important subject, because everybody's name is important. Everybody's name is important because it is our names which carry our reputations. It is by our names that we are known. Our names represent us. Therefore, we need to be careful how we handle somebody else's name.

❖ ❖ ❖ ❖ ❖
Identify the names of some well-known people (either from the present or from the past). Focus on their reputations. Especially focus on how what they did has given shape to their reputations. For what do you think people know you? What have you done which gives shape to your reputation? For what would you like people to know you? What happens when a person's reputation is damaged? Have you ever damaged somebody else's reputation? Has your reputation ever been damaged? What was the result of such damaging?
❖ ❖ ❖ ❖ ❖

God's reputation also travels on His name. Therefore, we should not take the name of the Lord our God in vain. That's what the Second Commandment tells us. You see, God's name which bears His reputation is not to be tossed about carelessly as if it doesn't amount to much. That is why we pray in the first petition of the Lord's Prayer, "God help us to hallow, to honor, Your name."

In his *Small Catechism* Martin Luther asks about this Petition:

What does this mean?

God's name is certainly holy in itself, but we pray in this petition that it may be kept holy among us also.

❖ ❖ ❖ ❖ ❖
"Hallowed" or "Holy" means "special," just as what God has done is special. What has God done that is so special? Make a list of things He has done for which God is so well-known.
❖ ❖ ❖ ❖ ❖

Certainly, God's name is holy. There is nothing that we can do to add to its holiness. Neither God nor His name is dependent upon us for that quality. However, that fact does not guarantee that we will always treat God or His name in a holy way. And that is why we begin this most important of all prayers praying that His name might be holy "among us." But ...

How is God's name kept holy?

God's name is kept holy when the Word of God is taught in its truth and purity, and we, as the children of God, also lead holy lives according to it. Help us to do this, dear Father in heaven! But anyone who teaches or lives contrary to God's Word profanes the name of God among us. Protect us from this, heavenly Father.

In other words, God's name is hallowed, is holy among us when we open our arms of faith to those words which tell us of what He has done for us. Those words then can mold and form our lives and give directions to our actions. That is what brings honor to God.

❖ ❖ ❖ ❖ ❖

Even though God's name is hallowed, holy, special all by itself, what are some of the ways in which we can make it special among us? Making His name so special among us can be very difficult. What are some of the things which inhibit and make such a hallowing difficult? Why do we find it difficult to hallow God's name? Do you see now why praying this petition is so important for members of the Family of God? Do you see how important it is for His reputation and for the reputation of His family?

❖ ❖ ❖ ❖ ❖

At the center of the First Petition then is what God has done for us. That is because what He has done for us is really the content of His reputation; His name carries the record of His actions. Hallowing God's name is holding before our eyes of faith the great acts of God which He has done on our behalf, and it is letting all of that give shape to how we live. Hallowing God's name is gathering around His Word so that we can remember Abraham, Isaac, Jacob, Noah, Moses, King David, King Hezekiah, Isaiah, Jeremiah, Ezekiel, Matthew, Mark, Luke, John, the Exodus, the Temple in Jerusalem, the cross on Calvary, and the Garden's empty tomb. Hallowing God's name is remembering how He has loved us through His Son, Jesus the Christ. Hallowing God's name is remembering His grace and mercy.

That, however, is not how his name is always remembered. That also is not how His name is sometimes used. Is it not true that God's name is often used to call down judgment upon the heads of those of whom we do not approve or upon those with whom we are angry? Cursing and damning, which is not our business, we sometimes make into our business. That, obviously, is far from hallowing God's name.

❖ ❖ ❖ ❖ ❖

What is the most important characteristic of God? (For what is God most well known?) Why is this the most important characteristic of God? What would be our condition and hope for the future if this was not the most important characteristic of God?

❖ ❖ ❖ ❖ ❖

In the Old Testament, the word for "hallowed" (or holy) comes from the Hebrew word *kadosh*. Kadosh means "to cut off, to separate from something else, to make what is cut off different, special." The point is that there is nothing which makes God more different than, separate from, everything else in this world than His grace and mercy. That is God's most important characteristic. Therefore, to hallow God's name means that we both publicly and privately remember His grace and mercy to others and to ourselves. It also means that we put into practice that same grace and mercy in our relationships with others and with ourselves. Instead of thinking of ourselves as executioners of God's wrath and anger, we find that we have become His ambassadors of peace. That is how we are to treat both ourselves and others. It is important for us to remember that.

In Exodus 20, at the time when the Ten Commandments were given, and again in Deuteronomy 5, at the time when Moses reviewed the Commandments for the people of Israel immediately before they entered the Promised Land, God said:

> *I the Lord your God am a jealous God, visiting the iniquity of the fathers upon the children to the third and the fourth generations of those who hate me, but showing steadfast love to thousands of those who love me and keep my commandments.*

❖ ❖ ❖ ❖ ❖

Refer to the chapter on the Conclusion to the Commandments. Why is it important for us that God's mercy "trump" His justice? Upon whom did the justice of God fully fall?

❖ ❖ ❖ ❖ ❖

Those words remind us that while God is a God of justice He is above all a God of mercy. That means that while on the one hand if God is any kind of God at all, He must stand for that which is proper and right, but on the other hand as a loving Father He is always ready and quick to forgive, to heal, and to restore. Yes, God must champion justice and what is right. And when what is right and just does not happen, He must do something more than just look the other way. If God is to be God, and if He is to be known to us as a father God, then there are times when He must as a father discipline us, His children. However, and this is the important point, it is also necessary that His discipline be interfered with, that is, if we are not going to be consumed by His anger. If we are going to have any kind of chance with God at all, His justice must be tempered.

❖ ❖ ❖ ❖ ❖

How important do you think it is for fathers (parents) to discipline their children? What would family life be like if there was no disciplining of children? But if fathers (parents) discipline their children, what must they also do? As a child, how important was that to you? If you are a parent, how important do you think that is to your child(ren)?

❖ ❖ ❖ ❖ ❖

Moses told us that if God's justice is carried to the third or fourth generation (to the third or fourth power), His mercy is extended to the thousandth generation (the one-thousandth power). That is a ratio of at least 250:1. The odds are clearly in our favor.

One of my favorite examples of this grace of God trumping his anger is found in the book of the Prophet Hosea.

> *How can I give you up, O Ephraim! How can I hand you over, O Israel! How can I make you like Admah! How can I treat you like Zeboim! My heart recoils within me,*

my compassion grows warm and tender. I will not execute my fierce anger. I will not again destroy Ephraim; for I am God and not man, the Holy One in your midst, and I will not come to destroy. — Hosea 11:8-9

The story presented by the Prophet Hosea was that of God being grieved. His heart had been pierced with sadness at the unfaithfulness of His people. (This story also reminds us of Jesus on Calvary.) If you or I had been God, we probably would have opted to clean up the whole mess with a snap of the fingers. A good thorough housecleaning would do the world some good. Why not condemn into oblivion all that which is evil and corrupt?

The world is filled with a lot of evil and with a lot of what is wrong. If you were God, how would you go about setting it right? How would you go about cleaning up all the evil that is so common? What kind of reputation would that give you? Do you think God's plan of loving and forgiving sinners is an effective plan? Does it work? Does it make the world a better place? What does that course of action do for God's reputation, His name?

But God's mercy trumps His justice, and that at a ratio of at least 250:1. And that, my friends, is what shows the hallowedness, the holiness of His name, more than anything else. His is a reputation known for its forgiveness; His is a reputation which proclaims new life. Thus, when His forgiveness abounds among us, then His name is holy among us. And we are also then called upon to make known everywhere that reputation.

Again, when something is holy (hallowed) it is different; it is special. How is the way God handles things different, special, holy, hallowed than the way the "world" would probably handle things? If God answers this prayer ("Hallowed be Thy name") for us as we pray it, how will how we handle things be different? What will that do for God's name (reputation) among us? Do you think we would have a better world?

This reminds me of a situation from one of William Shakespeare's plays, *Measure for Measure*. Claudio has been condemned to death by Angelo, the new and harsh ruler of Vienna. However, Claudio's sister, Isabella, pleads for his life. She asks that justice be suspended so that mercy might have its day. Her plea is made to the governor in this way:

Alas, alas. Why all the souls that were — were forfeit once; and he that might the vantage best have took found out the remedy. How would you be, if he, which is the top of judgment, should but judge you as you are? O, think on that, and mercy then will breathe within your lips like man new made.

Reconstruct in contemporary terms the scene from Shakespeare's *Measure for Measure* involving Claudio and Isabella and Angelo. What's the message here? Can you think of a situation in your family, in your church, in your community, in your school where mercy, not justice, had the last word? If so, what did that do for the situation and for the people involved?

❖ ❖ ❖ ❖ ❖

Isabella is saying that before God we all are condemned, even pious and righteous Angelo, the harsh ruler of Vienna. She even dared to say to him that if he got what he deserved, hell would be his fate. But God has mercy even on Angelo. Should that not then give him a new heart so that he in turn would have mercy on Isabella's brother, Claudio?

To hallow God's name, then, is to live and to say and to do as God lives, says, and does. That means that judgment does not have the last word. Mercy does! That is why we pray that we of His family, His children, might be more like Him, Our Father. In such a way is the guarantee of His reputation.

Questions

1. What is unique about the Lord's Prayer's use of pronouns? What is the significance of that?

2. What do our names carry?

3. What does the word "holy" in Hebrew mean?

4. The Old Testament's story of Hosea is parallel to what in the New Testament?

5. What is the nature of God's reputation?

6. What do we pray in the First Petition to be the nature of our reputations?

Discussion

1. Discuss ways in which you not only can but will hallow God's name.

2. Recall other incidents from history and literature which feature the quality of mercy.

The Lord's Prayer
The Second Petition

❖ ❖ ❖ ❖ ❖
When you hear the words "king" and "kingdom," what comes to mind? When you hear the word "king-size," what comes to mind? Why do you think that sometimes when we have the opportunity to ask for something, we are ready to settle for that which is regular in size instead of that which is king-sized?
❖ ❖ ❖ ❖ ❖

We come now to the Second Petition, the second prayer of the seven prayers that make up the most well-known of all prayers, the Lord's Prayer: "Thy Kingdom come."

Just three words: only four syllables in all. But no doubt about it; it is a KING-SIZE prayer. It is the prayer of the Kingdom, of the Kingdom of God. In it we are asking for the whole thing; we are asking for the whole kingdom of God to be right here, right with us, among us.

This second petition reminds me that often times our prayers really are not big enough. They are not king-size, or even queen-size, or even regular size. All too often we only ask for crumbs. How foolish to ask only for crumbs when we could have the whole loaf: the fare of the king's table, not just the crumbs that lie beneath it. So much is offered, yet we set our sights so low.

❖ ❖ ❖ ❖ ❖
As you read the story about Jacob and Esau (Genesis 27) ask yourself the questions, "What was Esau's main problem? Why did he trade so much for so little?" Have you ever found that your shortsightedness has led you to settle for a little when you could have had so much? If so, what were the circumstances? Would you agree that the press for

immediate gratification often stands in the way of looking for something bigger and better?

❖ ❖ ❖ ❖ ❖

That reminds me of a character from the Old Testament. His name was Esau. Esau loved to hunt. One day after being out on the hunt for a long time, he returned home to find his brother Jacob cooking some soup. The soup had a very appetizing aroma to it, so appetizing that Esau just could not control himself. He had to have some of this soup, and have it right now! Jacob, his brother, however, was a cunning sort of person. Thus, when Esau approached him and asked him for some of this soup, Jacob said that he would give some to Esau only if Esau, the older of the two brothers (actually, they were twins, but Esau had been born first) would bequeath him his entire birthright. That's driving a hard bargain. Nevertheless, Esau's hunger got the best of him, and he agreed. What a fool he was to give up so much for so little! Certainly, Jacob was not right in proposing such a bargain. He was not innocent in this affair. We cannot approve of his actions. But Esau was a fool for giving up so much for so little. He gave up the right to his father Isaac's property and wealth (which was considerable) for a bowl of soup.

That story reminds me of another one: a fable with a moral which I first heard when I was in kindergarten. Maybe you have heard it, too, when you were a youngster. It is the tale of a woodsman who set out to chop some wood. He approached a perfect-looking tree and was about to lay his axe to it when from out of the tree jumped one of those little elves that supposedly live in trees. This blithe spirit pleaded with the woodsman to spare the tree; it was his home. In exchange for the favor the elf promised that the woodsman could have any three wishes that he desired. Well, that seemed to be a good trade considering that there were many other trees in the forest which would serve for firewood just as well. So the deal was made.

Later that day, after working hard chopping down one tree after another, the woodsman returned home. He was hungry! However, when he asked his wife if supper was ready, she replied that it would be a little while. Whereupon the woodsman, his hunger getting the best of him, said, "I wish I had a plateful of sausage, right now!" Immediately there appeared before him a ring of the finest sausage you ever saw. His wife, startled by what had happened, asked him what this was all about. When he told her the story about the elf in the woods and the three wishes that had been promised to him, she immediately became indignant with him for making such a foolish and simple wish when he could have asked for anything in the whole world. Thus, in her anger, she became careless and said, "I wish that that sausage be strung through your nose. That's what you deserve, you fool." Whereupon the links of sausages became attached to the woodsman's nose like a brass ring through the nose of a bull. Well, that poor fellow was now in quite a fix. What was he to do? He had but one wish left. Yes, he had to use it right now. And it was so, and that was that, and that was the end of his three wishes, and that is the end of the story. The woodsman had traded away so much for so little.

The story about the woodsman and his three wishes is a classic story, although not many of us live in the woods and make our living by chopping down trees. Place this story into a modern setting. (In other words, rewrite it. Perhaps the setting could be in a store, a machine shop, or an office.) Does the rewritten story remind you of wasted opportunities? As members of the church, the Kingdom of God on earth, do we ever settle for so little when we could have had so much? Have we wasted opportunities? If you have witnessed that happening, what were the circumstances?

❖ ❖ ❖ ❖ ❖

"Lord, teach us to pray; teach us to pray that we don't ask for so little when you offer so much."

And He does teach us to pray, to say, "Father, Thy Kingdom come." And that is a lot more than just a bowl full of soup or a plate of sausage.

You might wonder, however, "Just what is the nature of this Kingdom for which we are urged to pray: What is it like?"

When you hear the words "Kingdom of God," what do you think? Describe your idea of that Kingdom. Where is it to be found? What makes it run? Who is in control? For what does it stand? How much power and influence does it have? Are you a part of it? If you are, are you comfortable being a part of it?

❖ ❖ ❖ ❖ ❖

The Scriptures give us the answer. In the record they have made of many of the parables that Jesus spoke, the Gospels give us a good description of this Kingdom. For example, in the thirteenth chapter of Matthew's Gospel we hear Jesus saying, "The Kingdom of God is like a treasure buried in a field. It is discovered by a man who then goes and sells all that he had in order to raise enough money to buy the field." Or, "the Kingdom is like a pearl, a pearl of great price. A buyer of pearls discovers it. He likewise sells everything else that he has so that he might have enough to buy this one pearl, greater in value than anything else."

In both cases, this treasure is more important to these men than anything else in the whole world. Certainly, to them the Kingdom of God (the treasure in the field and the pearl) is something of far more value than a bowl of soup or a plateful of sausage. For that matter, the Kingdom is greater than ALL the bowls of soup and all of the sausages in the whole world.

❖ ❖ ❖ ❖ ❖
When you pray to God, for what do you most frequently ask? Have you ever seriously meant it when you prayed, "Thy Kingdom come"? Why is it a risky thing to really mean it when you pray that petition?
❖ ❖ ❖ ❖ ❖

That precisely is the point. Be careful: don't think that the Kingdom of God is a bowl of soup or a link of sausage. The Kingdom of God is not to be confused with the things of this world. For example, it is not uncommon these days to hear the instruction, "Ask God for a blessing; expect a miracle." We are urged to pray for health and wealth, for security and success, for fame, ease, and leisure. We are told that God wants us to have these things. All you have to do is ask and believe, and He will give. But if that is all we expect of the King, then we have made out of Him a mere "bread king"; then we have relegated Him to the soup kitchen. Meanwhile, He has invited us to ask for a lot more; He has invited us to ask for the whole Kingdom.

The whole Kingdom, however, might not be that which we want. It might be more than what we want. Because, you see, inviting the Kingdom of God into our lives means that we are inviting God's way of living into our lives. And that is exactly what Martin Luther put his thumb on when in his explanation to the Second Petition he wrote in the *Small Catechism*:

> *The kingdom of God certainly comes by itself without our prayer, but we pray in this petition that it may come to us also.*
>
> *How does God's kingdom come?*
>
> *God's kingdom comes when our heavenly Father gives us His Holy Spirit, so that by His grace we believe His holy Word and lead godly lives here in time and there in eternity.*

❖ ❖ ❖ ❖ ❖
Usually when we think of a kingdom and a king, we think of someone who has power and authority over the lives of his subjects, those who live in his kingdom. Why might we be hesitant in asking God to be such a king over us? What might it mean as far as our lifestyles are concerned?
❖ ❖ ❖ ❖ ❖

The Kingdom of God, you see, is a way of life more than it is a place or even made up of things. Therefore, many of the parables which Jesus told about the Kingdom of God had to do with a whole new way of living, with a whole new way of looking at one's self and at one's neighbor. And it is precisely that Kingdom which might not be in popular demand.

For example, when we pray "Thy Kingdom come" we are praying that God's mind be our mind. In Luke 15 we have three examples of that. This chapter of parables begins with Luke telling us about "a Good Shepherd." The Good Shepherd does not rest until he has found the one sheep that has wandered away from the 99. If any of us had been that shepherd, we probably would have just forgotten about the one sheep that was lost. It was the sheep's fault that it was lost in the first place, and it probably was a troublemaker, not worth retrieving.

> Read the entire fifteenth chapter of Luke's Gospel. What does it have to say about the nature of God's Kingdom? For what is it well known? What effect should that have on the lives of those who are citizens of His Kingdom? Do you see now how in praying the Second Petition of the Lord's Prayer we are asking for something far more than just an item or two? Is it not true that we are praying for a whole new way of living, a new life? How would you describe this whole new way of living? (Refer to Galatians 3:22ff. What do such words as love, joy, peace, and so forth mean?) Can you think of any other sections of Scripture which describe what "Kingdom living" is like?

Luke follows that parable with the one in which Jesus tells about a housewife who, having lost one coin, turns her house upside down until she has found it. (Who among us would go to such pains?)

These two parables are followed by the parable of the Prodigal Son, or as I like to call it, "The Parable of the Father of Prodigals." Even though I, too, am a father, I have a hard time thinking like the father in this story. He is so good, so gracious, so forgiving.

But that's it! That is the nature of Kingdom living. The father sets the example for all of us to be known also for our grace and mercy and forgiveness. The story of the Father being that way toward us is "The Greatest Story Ever Told," and it is a story worth retelling, worth reliving by His Kingdom people.

"Thy Kingdom come" is our praying that we might live as people of God's Kingdom of grace, that even as we have received so we might give. That's the First Article of the Kingdom's constitution. Even as the founding fathers of this nation proclaimed "these truths to be self-evident, that all men are created equal," and upon that premise built everything else in their new political system, so also upon the self-evident principle of God's goodness is everything else in His Kingdom built. This is the foundation of the Kingdom of God, and when we pray for it, we pray a prayer big enough to hold everything else that might also be said.

> Review the Declaration of Independence of the United States. It contains principles upon which the Constitution was built. Identify some

> of those principles and how they have given shape to the government of the United States. Now identify some of the principles upon which life within the Kingdom of God is built (to be lived).

❖ ❖ ❖ ❖ ❖

Jesus did say other things about the Kingdom, particularly in Matthew 22 and 25. In Chapter 22 the Kingdom is compared to a wedding feast to which many people are invited. However, many turn down the invitation. In addition, some who came to the wedding refused to wear the festive garments provided by the king. What do you think that has to say about Kingdom living?

❖ ❖ ❖ ❖ ❖

> Chapters 13, 22, and 25 are Matthew's great Kingdom chapters. Read the numerous Kingdom parables which Jesus told. What do they have to say about the nature of Kingdom living now? If you really mean it when you pray the Second Petition, what could you expect as far as your life is concerned?

❖ ❖ ❖ ❖ ❖

In Chapter 25 the Kingdom is compared to a wedding procession for which, if one wanted to be a part, he or she had only to be ready. Further on in that same chapter, Jesus compared Kingdom living with stewardship, the citizens of the Kingdom properly applying themselves to the responsibilities which had been entrusted to them. What do you think that has to say about Kingdom living?

I could go on and on, talking about Kingdom living, but the concluding point that I want to make is that, as you can see, Kingdom business is big business. It surely is large enough. It is a way of life for which we pray in the Second Petition of the Lord's Prayer, a prayer addressed to large enough God for a large enough life, a life which is made up of a lot more than just soup and sausage.

When we pray "Thy Kingdom come" we pray that our minds might be like God's mind, the mind of the King. We pray that the way He does things would be the way we do things. Living that way means that we would be a part of that Kingdom now and forever.

Questions

1. What was Esau's problem?

2. What was the woodsman's problem?

3. To what did Jesus compare the Kingdom of God?

4. What is the First Article of the Kingdom of God's constitution?

Discussion

1. Relate the story of Esau and the woodsman to prayers which have too narrow of a focus.

2. Describe the Kingdom of God as you see it.

3. If you really take praying the Second Petition seriously, what impact could that have on your life?

The Lord's Prayer
The Third Petition

Have you ever heard it said or said it yourself: "It must have been the will of the Lord"? Surely, you have heard it. Surely, you have said it. We have all heard it, and we have all said it, probably many times.

❖ ❖ ❖ ❖ ❖

In your own experience, what are some of the bad things that have happened at which time someone said, "It must have been the will of the Lord"?

❖ ❖ ❖ ❖ ❖

When something bad happens in life, when something happens which is hard to explain, when it is difficult to see the reason behind why something happened, we are all quite quick to throw up our hands and say, "Well, it must have been the will of the Lord." Consequently, God gets blamed for a lot of things. For example, when someone near to us has died of some dreadful disease, we are apt to say, "It must have been the will of the Lord. How else can you explain it?" Or let's say that a person is forced to live under horrible circumstances in a home where either husband or wife or perhaps child is irresponsible and by his or her behavior brings all kinds of hurt and heartache. In the face of such a situation we also are apt to say that God must have a hand in it and is laying a cross upon the shoulders of the rest of the members of the family. Yes, it must be God's will. The same goes for traffic accidents and madman maniacs, too. Therefore, it can be assumed that God is responsible for the Hitlers of this world and nuclear accidents and famine.

Yes, God does get blamed for all sorts of bad things that happen in life, ranging all the way from tornadoes and earthquakes (we even call them "Acts of God"), to cancer and famine, to irresponsible behavior on the part of immature people and the anger of those who cannot control their tempers or who are simply out of their minds.

Why do you think insurance companies use the term "act of God" when referring to a natural disaster? Why do you think that there are natural disasters? (Check Genesis 3 and Romans 8:18-23.) If what Paul says in Romans 13 about governments is true, can God also be held responsible for the likes of Adolf Hitler?

That makes God out to be some sort of maniac Himself then, doesn't it? A god who acts capriciously, at random, striking at both nature and people, apparently delighting in seeing us wiggle and squirm, must be some sort of monster God.

If we are uncomfortable with that, then we can go to the other extreme. Perhaps as a reaction to the absurd blaming of God that some people do, others simply remove God from any sense of responsibility at all. They simply take God out of the picture completely. Consequently, they put God so far from the course of human affairs and the turning of the world that He counts for nothing at all. His will and His willing are simply discounted. For all practical intents and purposes, God now ceases to exist. God is dead, or at least He is not a force with which to be reckoned.

Do you think that God can make a thunderstorm quiet? Do you think that He can turn the course of a hurricane? Can God send rain or sunshine at will? If He can, does He? Do people who pray at the time of illness experience any greater degree of health than people who do not pray? If they do, is the benefit a result of their praying or of God answering? If God does not take an active role in the affairs of humankind and the earth, does that indicate that either He does not exist or that He just doesn't care?

If this is true, or if that is true, then what can we say about the will of God? On the one hand, it seems improper and foolish to blame Him for everything that goes wrong, and on the other hand, it seems equally as improper and foolish to take Him completely out of the picture. Just what then is the will of the Lord? What do we mean when in the Third Petition of the Lord's Prayer we pray, "Thy will be done"?

The power of the will is said to be a great power. One best-selling book of several decades ago was titled *The Power of Positive Thinking*. Even football coaches tell their players that the game is twenty percent talent and eighty percent a matter of the mind, of the will. Today we are also told that we can accomplish whatever we want if only we will it

hard enough. What do you think about the power of the will, about willpower? How strong is it? What can it do? Does it have any limits?

❖ ❖ ❖ ❖ ❖

To catch a clue for the answer, let's look at what the catechism of Martin Luther has to say about the question. In response to the Third Petition, the third prayer of the Lord's Prayer, he asks:

What does this mean?

The good and gracious will of God is done even without our prayer, but we pray in this petition that it may be done among us also.

How is God's will done?

God's will is done when He breaks and hinders every evil plan and purpose of the devil, the world, and our sinful nature, which do not want us to hallow God's name or let His kingdom come; and when He strengthens and keeps us firm in His Word and faith until we die. This is His good and gracious will.

God does what He wills; He is not open to manipulation. Tugging at His shirt sleeve is not going to help us get our way with Him. But we pray in this prayer that His will will be our will! We pray that God would have His way with us. We pray that we would see the wisdom in what God wishes and wants and wills to such a degree that we too, without coercion or threat, might wish and want and will the same.

❖ ❖ ❖ ❖ ❖

Many times it is said that a person is "stubborn." A stubborn person often just will not budge. A stubborn person has his or her mind made up and will not change it. Do you think that the Third Petition is aimed at stubbornness? If you do, at what kind of stubbornness is it taking aim?

❖ ❖ ❖ ❖ ❖

This is something much more than merely acquiescing, giving in to the inevitable, that which is stronger and mightier than what we are. This petition, "Thy will be done," is not a prayer of resignation. Rather, it is a prayer of excitement, of possibilities, of new horizons, of God's will becoming our very own, of our will becoming like God's will.

That is asking for quite a bit, because by nature our wills are at odds with God's will. Even the Bible is loaded with examples of just that: God willing one thing and people like you and me willing something altogether different or holding back from volunteering to do God's will. Think of Moses. He ran for his life into the Sinai wilderness. There, as he wandered around, not really knowing what to do, God appeared to him in a flaming bush. Obviously, Moses was quite startled by the whole affair. If you or I had been in his shoes (which, by the way, he had to take off in the presence of the Almighty because the ground upon which he was standing was holy ground), would we have been any more responsive? Or would we have protested like he protested? At any rate, the Lord told him, "Go tell Pharaoh to let my people go." Moses shook his head, "No." There was no way that he was going to go back to Egypt. Under no circumstances. And then he began to give excuses: "Who should I tell them has sent me? God? They are not going to believe me."

❖ ❖ ❖ ❖ ❖
Moses did not want to give in to God. What were some of his reasons? Do you think that they were good reasons? Would you have reacted like Moses did?
❖ ❖ ❖ ❖ ❖

But God simply said to Moses, "Yes, tell them that God has sent you. Tell them that I Am Who I Am, YAHWEH, the God of Abraham, Isaac, and Jacob has sent you."

Moses was quick on the draw, even as we so often are when it comes to things like this. He had an excuse. He said, "When I tell them that, they will just laugh and say that I've been dreaming again, or maybe that I am a little sunstruck, having been out here in the desert so long. I'll have to have proof that you talked to me. It is hard to convince others if you have had only a 'one-man vision.' "

❖ ❖ ❖ ❖ ❖
"Giving in" is sometimes equated with weakness. It is considered to be a negative behavior and not very desirable. Do you think that "giving in" should be avoided at all costs? When might you give in to God? When might you give in to another person?
❖ ❖ ❖ ❖ ❖

God was just as quick as was Moses — even quicker. He presented to him a rod, a staff, a walking stick that had miraculous powers. When thrown onto the ground it became a snake. When dipped in water it changed that water into blood. When waved over a vast sea, it separated the waters of the sea so that a dry road ran straight between walls of water on each side.

Needless to say, Moses was quite impressed. After all, a burning bush, a voice from heaven, and now a miraculous walking stick. But he still held back. He still did not want to do what God wanted him to do. He still had a mind of his own. He was not about to say, "Lord, Thy will be done here on earth and in Egypt as you have willed it in heaven." He protested once more. "Bbbbut, IIIII, ccccannnnn't ttttalk wwwwwell. IIIII ssssstttttuuuttttter. Ppppppphaaroah and all the pppppppeople wwwwill lllllaugh aaat mmmme." To which the Lord responded with a double-barreled retort: "I'll put the words into your mouth, and I'll help you to say them. In addition, I'll send your brother Aaron with you. You know how he likes to talk."

❖ ❖ ❖ ❖ ❖
To have opposing wills seems to be natural. Everybody has his or her own agenda and strives to see that it gets done. What are some of the competing agendas that exist in your family, between you and your friends, within your community, and throughout the nation (like Republicans and Democrats have their different agendas)? Sometimes we are told that the best remedy to these kinds of situations is compromise. When are some good times for compromise? When are some times when compromise might not be so good?

Only after this did Moses change his mind. He then decided that the will of God would be his will. It was not easy for him. There were even many more times still to come when he certainly had his doubts. Did he really want his will to be the same as God's will?

Jesus, Himself, had to struggle with this. Remember how it was with Him in the Garden of Gethsemane just three hours before he was arrested and led away to be crucified? He was staring death straight in the eye, and He didn't like what He saw. Three times on His knees He prayed. Those prayers were an hour long each. With sweat that seemed like great drops of blood on His forehead, He prayed: "Father, if it be Thy will, let this cup of suffering pass from me, for that's what I would like. Nevertheless, not my will but your will be done — by me." Jesus was tempted to hold back. As a human He did not want to die, especially did He not want to die in disgrace.

❖ ❖ ❖ ❖ ❖
Count how many seconds it takes to say the words that Jesus prayed in the Garden of Gethsemane. How is it possible that it took Jesus an hour each of the three times He prayed that prayer? With what kind of activity do you think Jesus filled the rest of the hour? What does this have to say to us about the nature of prayer? Do you think that the Holy Spirit really does talk to us in the quiet moments of our prayers? Why is it important for us to have some time in our prayers when we are quiet?
❖ ❖ ❖ ❖ ❖

That incident in the Garden of Gethsemane goes to show us how great the tension can sometimes get between our will and God's will. Even Jesus had to wrestle with that.

Do you think it strange that Jesus had to wrestle with the heavenly Father in prayer? Why do you think that He had to pray like He did in the Garden of Gethsemane?

What was at stake at that moment when Jesus prayed on the Mount of Olives? What if Jesus had not done the Father's will but instead had opted for His own safety?

❖ ❖ ❖ ❖ ❖

In that Garden the salvation of the whole world was at stake. None of us can ever say that the battles between our wills and God's are that great, that important. So maybe if we don't do His will, if we hold back a little every now and then, it won't be so bad, and the consequences won't be so severe. And I suppose that is true. But that is also just another excuse not to deal with God's will in our lives.

So, Lord, teach us to pray as the disciples asked you to teach them to pray. Take us to the Garden of Gethsemane along with you that we might learn what it is like to seek God the Father's will.

Yes, Jesus' experience in the Garden of Gethsemane ought to be our experience every night and every day as we, disciples, not being above the Master, pray with Him that we might be agents of the Father's will, hallowing His name, and being instruments for the coming of His Kingdom. "This is His good and gracious will."

❖ ❖ ❖ ❖ ❖

How difficult is it for you to do God's will? What is God's will for you? What are some of the things which get in the way of your doing God's will? How can you overcome those things which stand in the way of your doing God's will?

❖ ❖ ❖ ❖ ❖

Questions

1. For what does God often get blamed?

2. Instead of blaming God for bad things that happen, what do some people do?

3. For what did Jesus pray in the Garden of Gethsemane?

Discussion

1. Discuss with others what you see as God's will for your life.

2. Discuss situations in which you protested God having His way with you. Why do we so often resist God's will?

The Lord's Prayer
The Fourth Petition

❖ ❖ ❖ ❖ ❖
Wherever civilization developed, it was around the cultivation of grain which was made into bread. The first evidence of the cultivation of grain which was then made into bread was at Jarmo, in the borderland region of the foothills of the Zagros Mountains between Iraq and Iran. Look for that region on a map. Think also of museum displays you have seen of early and primitive civilizations. Do you remember the role that grain harvesting and breadmaking played in those civilizations? No wonder bread has been named "the staff of life."
❖ ❖ ❖ ❖ ❖

Anybody can ask for bread. You don't even have to be religious to ask for bread, for daily bread.

Bread, sometimes referred to as the "staff of life," is also that which represents all that we need to stay alive, all that which nurtures and nourishes the body. Bread: all the way from wheat and rye to underwear and overalls to sunshine and black dirt. Anybody can ask for it. Indeed, we all have been doing just that ever since our first peep: "Mom, I'm cold. Mom, will you please cover me?" (After all, a 25 degree drop in temperature in just a few minutes is a big drop for a body without any clothes on.) And then came, "Mom, I'm hungry. Mom, I'm wet." And so it goes: "Give us this day our daily bread — all that we need from day to day. Abba Father in heaven, give us what we need to live."

❖ ❖ ❖ ❖ ❖
Do you pray "table prayers" so that you can have more bread? Do you think that you would have just as much bread if you didn't pray for it?

Do you notice any difference when you don't pray a table prayer from when you do? Why pray for daily bread anyway? What good does it do?

Do you pray a table prayer when you are in public? Have you seen others pray in public, at a restaurant or at school? Why might you hesitate from praying a table prayer in public? What comes to mind when you see someone praying in public?

I remember hearing a story when I was in grade school. That was right after World War II. At that time everybody was afraid that the communists were going to take over the world and outlaw religion. The story was about schoolchildren in Poland. During the last days of the war the Russian communists had invaded and occupied Poland. One of the noteworthy things about the Polish people then as now is that they were very religious. Therefore, before lunch was served in school every day, the children would pray a table prayer. "Our Father who art in heaven, give us this day our daily bread." Such a prayer, however, was unacceptable to the communists who had taken control of things, including the schools. These communists also were atheists. That meant that they did not believe in God, an "Our Father" kind or any other kind. Therefore, the children were instructed, "Bread does not come from God. Instead it comes by the good graces of comrade Joseph Stalin." He was at that time the leader of the communist world. "You must ask him for daily bread, and then you shall have it."

"Oh no," came the response of the children. "We must pray to God, our Father in heaven, for daily bread."

"Well then, you pray to Him and see how much bread you get."

The children continued to pray each day before lunch, "Our Father, who art in heaven ... Give us this day our daily bread."

None came. No lunch was placed before the children.

Finally, their new communist leaders said, "Now you ask comrade Stalin in Moscow, and you shall have bread."

The near-starving children petitioned Joseph Stalin for bread, and, lo and behold, it was immediately placed before them. The new communist teachers were sure that their pupils had learned their lesson well. (Apparently not, however, for the Polish people to this day are the most religious of all the peoples of Europe, and that in spite of decades of atheistic government.)

Although it is not included in the story, what do you think those Polish children did after they received their daily bread from their communist rulers?

Is it harder to pray in a free country where you are permitted to pray or to pray in a country where you are told not to pray? Why do you think the way you do about this?

❖ ❖ ❖ ❖ ❖

What does this mean for us? It means that the Fourth Petition of the Lord's Prayer is a prayer of faith, of trust, that God will one way or the other provide enough bread each day for kingdom living. He will do it!

❖ ❖ ❖ ❖ ❖

The story of God providing food for the Israelites while they were in the wilderness places emphasis upon the "daily" part of the prayer: "give us this day our DAILY bread." Why do you suppose they were instructed not to take more than what they needed for just one day? Compare this story with the parable Jesus told in Luke 12:13-21. What do you think is the "moral" of these two stories?

❖ ❖ ❖ ❖ ❖

A good example of this recorded in the Scriptures is the incident found in Exodus 16. The Israelites had just crossed the Sea of Reeds, the Red Sea, into the Sinai Peninsula. They were barely a couple of weeks out of Egypt, and then they ran out of bread. They became hungry. They moaned and groaned to and against Moses, saying that they would have been better off "red than dead" — that is, in Egypt as slaves but alive instead of being out there in the desert starving to death. They were sure that they would have been better off in their old way of life instead of being out there in the wilderness, free but dying of hunger.

God heard their complaint, and He also saw their plight. So He told Moses to tell the people that each morning He would provide for them a sweet-tasting bread called "manna." All that they would have to do was pick it up off the ground. Each evening He would send flocks of quail into their camp. All that they would have to do is just pluck them out of their air. This bread and this meat would be for their taking. However, this caution was made: They were not to take any more than enough for one day at a time. The one exception was on the day before the Sabbath. Then they could take twice as much, enough for two days, because on the Sabbath there would be no manna in the morning and no quail in the evening.

There was also a warning: If anyone cheated and took more than enough for one day, if anyone got greedy, if anyone doubted the promise and thought, "I might as well take all that I can get while the taking is good because I can't be sure about tomorrow," whatever was left from one day to the next quickly spoiled. It became like garbage, uneatable, a nuisance. It had to be disposed of, to the embarrassment of the greedy ones, the faithless ones.

❖ ❖ ❖ ❖ ❖

In his *Large Catechism*, while commenting on the First Commandment, Martin Luther, in answer to the question "What is God?" said, "A god is that to which we look for all good and in which we find refuge in every time of need." Do you think that there is a connection between the First Commandment and the Fourth Petition of the Lord's Prayer? What is the connection? Refer now also to the First Article of the Apostles' Creed. Is there a connection between it and the Fourth Petition? What is the connection?

❖ ❖ ❖ ❖ ❖

Do you see what the point was? It was to be a matter of trust, of trust that God would provide His people each day with that which was necessary for them to do what He had chosen them to do. That is why we come to the conclusion that praying "Give us this day our daily bread" is a prayer of trust that God will provide for our daily needs as His Kingdom people so that we might get on with hallowing His name and with the doing of His will. We are not to worry about how much bread we can store. As Jesus said in Matthew 6:

> ... *do not be anxious, saying, "What shall we eat?" or "What shall we drink?" or "What shall we wear?" For the Gentiles seek all these things; and your heavenly Father knows that you need them all. But seek first His kingdom and His righteousness, and all these things shall be yours as well.*

Such a posture of the heart will allow us to receive our "daily" bread with "thanks." That's what Martin Luther thought was the most important thing about this petition.

Some people think that happiness and thankfulness go together. Do you think happiness precedes thankfulness or that thankfulness precedes happiness? Is there a cause and effect relationship here?

❖ ❖ ❖ ❖ ❖

However, that is not the way it always is. For example, children (and adults, too) often complain about the way the soup tastes; they complain about the salad. There is all too often all too much which does not meet with their approval. Parents then think that their brood is altogether ungrateful instead of being thankful that they have something to eat. In fact, some of those parents can even remember when and where there was not too much of anything to eat. Therefore, they wish that their children would be more thankful, more grateful.

Not only does the Fourth Petition urge us to pray daily for our daily bread, but it also urges us to be thankful daily. Why is that important?

Have you ever become dissatisfied with your daily bread? What does that dissatisfaction do to you? What kind of person does it make you? Are you then pleasant to be around? Does your dissatisfaction have any effect on those around you? What does that kind of attitude have to say about your being a part of the Kingdom? What effect does it have on your Kingdom living? If we are not worried about tomorrow, what can we do today?

❖ ❖ ❖ ❖ ❖

For the children of the heavenly Father it is often much the same. Often we too, like the Israelites in the wilderness, complain about our daily bread and forget why it is being given to us in the first place. The Israelites even went so far as to complain about the manna, which was like wafers made of coriander seed and honey — probably very tasty. That complaining is a problem, isn't it? That is why it is important for us to pray each day to the heavenly Father that we would receive our daily bread with thanks. "Lead us into saying, 'Thank you,' Lord." Translated into daily living that means saying as we sit at breakfast or lunch or dinner, "O give thanks unto the Lord for He is good, for His mercy endures forever." Or it might mean simply saying, "We thank the Lord for all this food, for life and health and every good." Only fifteen words: that's all. But, oh, how important.

Therefore, we pray the Fourth Petition of the Lord's Prayer as an act of faith, an act of trust; we are sure that God will provide each day our daily bread for His Kingdom living. We ask for no more. In fact, in our asking we are automatically drawing limits. We are not concerned about laying up for ourselves treasures for the future. Instead, we are saying, "Help us, Father, not to be too worried about tomorrow. Help us not to be greedy. Help us to be satisfied with the bread we have for today so that today we can live as your kingdom people, doing your will, participating in the coming of your kingdom, and hallowing your name. Help us to understand that because of your goodness there will be more for tomorrow when tomorrow comes." In addition we are also saying, "Thank you, God."

So we trust, and so we give thanks, because we are Children of the Kingdom. And it is in our breaking of the bread which comes from the King that we recognize the King and Kingdom living. For example, when Jesus, shortly after His resurrection, walked to Emmaus with two of His disciples, they did not recognize Him until He sat at the supper table with them and broke bread. Then, we are told, they recognized Him in that breaking of the bread — in the thankful eucharistic sharing of the bread.

Some think that the Emmaus Easter story is the best of all the Easter stories (Luke 24:13-35). Read it. What is so important about this story? Do you think that Christ can really be recognized in the breaking and sharing of daily bread? Do you see any connection between that and

the bread of Holy Communion? (Holy Communion is also known as the Eucharist. The word "Eucharist" means "giving thanks: thanksgiving.") How is the bread of Holy Communion important for daily living of the Kingdom life? Do you recognize a spirit of thankfulness when people receive Holy Communion at your church?

❖ ❖ ❖ ❖ ❖

The bread for which we pray is also a bread which is to be shared. It is a sign of the Kingdom God among us. That is why we pray for our daily bread, and why we receive it with thanks. It then becomes an instrument by which we share this Kingdom with others. "Give us this day our daily bread" is a petition in which we ask the heavenly Father to open our hearts so that as we share our daily bread with others we might also share with them the Bread of Life, He who is the Staff of Eternal Life.

As Martin Luther reminds us in the *Small Catechism*, God feeds all of his creatures. But the reason why he feeds those who are of His kingdom is altogether different than the reason why he feeds the squirrels. We pray in this petition that we may be led to realize that. God gives daily bread to us for a special reason; it is no longer there just to keep us alive.

❖ ❖ ❖ ❖ ❖

Martin Luther insists that God does everything for a purpose. For what purpose does He give you daily bread? For what purpose do you receive your daily bread with thanksgiving?

❖ ❖ ❖ ❖ ❖

May God bless us with daily bread. May we receive it with thanks and, because of it, be a blessing to others as we share with them the Staff of Life which is a sign of the Kingdom.

Questions

1. What is regarded as the "staff of life"?

2. For what do we pray in the Fourth Petition?

3. With what did God provide the Israelites as they journeyed through the Sinai wilderness?

4. What would happen if they hoarded more than a day's provision?

5. Of what is the breaking of bread among Christians a sign?

Discussion

1. Discuss why and how the Fourth Petition is a prayer of trust. Use examples from your own life experiences.

2. Discuss the purpose and reason for praying the Fourth Petition.

The Lord's Prayer
The Fifth Petition

❖ ❖ ❖ ❖ ❖
It seems that wherever people are, pollution occurs. What are some examples of pollution caused by people? Can we ever be pollution free? If pollution is inevitable, what must be done with all that stuff that accumulates and fouls up the place? Is sin inevitable? If it is, what must be done with it so that it doesn't foul up one's entire life? In other words, what is the proper response to sin, to it being all around us? There are, after all, a number of possible ways to respond to it. What are some of those ways? What ways are inappropriate? What is the only way in which the problem can be handled in a healthy manner?
❖ ❖ ❖ ❖ ❖

I once knew a lady who never cleaned her house. It got so bad around her that after a while even she could not stand the smell anymore. Just too much garbage. So she burned down her house. Of course, that didn't really solve her problem. Yes, she got rid of her garbage for a while. But then she didn't have a place to live. It really wasn't her fault. She didn't ask for all of that garbage. But I suppose that wherever she eventually did find another place to live, the garbage built up there, too. Perhaps by now she has burned down that house also.

I don't really want to talk about garbage, but what I have on my mind is something similar. It's sin. I really don't want to talk about sin either. Sin and garbage are awful stuff, and both, if allowed to accumulate, really do foul up our lives. That is why we pray in the Fifth Petition of the Lord's Prayer, "Father, forgive us our trespasses (our sins, our debts), as we forgive those who trespass against us." That means, "Father, remove all this garbage which is our sin." That really is what I want to talk to you about: forgiveness, forgiveness of sins.

In his explanation to the Fifth Petition, Martin Luther wrote:

We pray in this petition that our Father in heaven would not look at our sins, or deny our prayer because of them. We are neither worthy of the things for which we pray, nor have we deserved them, but we ask that He would give them all to us by grace, for we daily sin much and surely deserve nothing but punishment. So we too will sincerely forgive and gladly do good to those who sin against us.

In some respects we can say that the Fifth Petition of the Lord's Prayer is the heart and soul of the entire prayer. We can say that because if God is not willing to forgive us then all the other things for which we pray in this prayer are beyond reach and possibility. If God does not forgive us, God will have nothing to do with us. If there is no forgiveness, then there is no power for the hallowing of His Name, then there will be no chance of the living of the Kingdom Life, then there will be no willing for doing His will, and there will be no reason for receiving daily bread with thanksgiving. Indeed, if there is no forgiveness, then all that there is, all that there will be, is garbage. Yes, we might learn to live with a lot of garbage around the house for a while. But if the place smells badly enough, sooner or later nobody else is going to come around for a visit. Nobody will want to live there either. Yes, we simply must get rid of the garbage.

Sin is a lot like that. It too must be removed. It must be removed even if we are not always sensitive to it being around, to it accumulating around our feet, to it spreading up to our knees; it must be removed even when we are not aware of our sinking into it up to our necks, and even when it is about to completely smother us.

Why do you think we need help and guidance in praying for forgiveness? Why might we be hesitant in asking for forgiveness? Could it have to do with our thinking that what we did is not so bad or, just the opposite, is it so bad that forgiveness would not be appropriate?

Why do you think we need help and guidance in praying that we would be forgiving of others? Why is it hard to sometimes forgive someone? Do you think that forgiving is a sign of permissiveness? Does forgiveness, especially if it is easily and freely given, lead to more sin?

Thus when with the disciples we ask Jesus, "Teach us to pray," essential to our request must be the petition in which we ask for instruction on how to pray for forgiveness. "Father, forgive us our trespasses." Those words are essential; they are the essence of living with God. Indeed, upon the foundation of forgiveness, everything else is built.

"Easy come, easy go" means that if something is too easy it has little value. Do you think that is always true? Or, "You only get what you

pay for." Do you think that is always true? Do these cliches have anything at all to do with forgiveness? How serious does God take sin to be? How hard was it for Him to be forgiving of us? What did it cost Him?

❖ ❖ ❖ ❖ ❖

One of the wonderful things about the Gospel is that this forgiveness for which we pray is not just the sounding of words. You know what I mean. Oftentimes we find ourselves in a situation where in order to keep peace, or because we are pressured into it, we might rather routinely "forgive" somebody. The hope is that a difficult circumstance might go away without too much effort; perhaps just a few kind words will take care of the problem. So we say, "All right, I forgive you. Forget it. It's okay." It might be, however, that our hearts are not really in those words. We might merely be going through the motions. God, however, when He forgives, is not merely going through the motions. His heart is in it. The life and death of Jesus Christ, the Son of God, is His testimony to that. Saint Paul said that "He became sin for us, even though He knew no sin, so that we might become the righteousness of God." That is to be understood literally, because it is something that has really happened. Nobody could ever take forgiveness any more seriously than that. God Himself took on Himself our flesh and came among us, among our garbage, in order to remove it from us as far as the east is from the west.

❖ ❖ ❖ ❖ ❖

What might be a circumstance in which forgiving another person would not be easy for you to do? What might be a circumstance in which forgiving another person might cost you dearly?

❖ ❖ ❖ ❖ ❖

I suppose that all sorts of little stories have been told in order to help us grasp and appreciate this. Here is one: It is about two GIs in the same foxhole in France during World War II. They had both crawled into it after a fierce but unsuccessful assault on an enemy position. During the assault one of them had been severely injured. The other soldier was untouched. The wounded GI, who knew that he would soon die, said to the other: "Hey Joe, you've had a tough time of it, a rough life. You know, with your prison record and all. They'll never let you forget that. It will follow you all of your life. I have no record. I've never served time, except here in the army. There are no convictions against me. There's nothing on the books against my name. I'll give you my name. You can start all over again with a clean record. Here, take my dog tag, and you give me yours. Your record will die with me."

Jesus says to us: "Here, take my life. I give it to you. And you, you hand over to me your life so that I can carry all of your sins away. Here, take my name. Straight off you'll have no more convictions."

That is complete and absolute forgiveness. It is unconditional.

❖ ❖ ❖ ❖ ❖
Unconditional forgiveness with no limits is quite something. Think of a "sinful" circumstance which is so bad that you might like to draw some limits and set some conditions. Think of a "sinful" circumstance which might not be as bad, but which in your estimation would still warrant some limits or conditions. Do we have the tendency to keep some strings attached to forgiveness?
❖ ❖ ❖ ❖ ❖

You might ask, however, "Why is it then that in the Fifth Petition we ask, 'Forgive us as we forgive those who trespass against us'?" That sounds conditional. That sounds as if we are saying, "God, you go as far with us as we are willing to go with each other." That sounds as if God's forgiving of us is to be conditioned upon our forgiving one another. That, however, is not for what we are really praying. The problem is that the limits of language sometimes interfere with the meaning of language. Therefore, I suppose that if we were to rewrite this prayer in a way which gives good expression to what we mean, it would sound more like this: "Father, help us to forgive others as you have forgiven us." You see, our forgiving of others is always predicated upon our first being the forgiven ones. Being forgiven, we can then be forgiving.

❖ ❖ ❖ ❖ ❖
There are two very strong forces in this world: 1) to be ordered to do something (to do something because you HAVE to do it), and 2) to do something out of love (to do something because you WANT to do it). Which force do you think is the stronger? Does being forgiven make it any easier to be forgiving?
❖ ❖ ❖ ❖ ❖

There is a risk involved here. It is risky business being a garbage man, like the kind Jesus was. It cost Him His life. Some cynics might say, "Well, that goes with the territory." Yes, indeed, it does. Do you remember what I said before about this forgiveness business being more than just empty words? It is also action, deeds, lives. It is very costly. If we are really serious about hallowing His name, if we are really serious about being a part of His Kingdom coming, then we must take up this business of forgiving others even as we have been forgiven, and we have to really be serious about it. That is because we now know how important it is. It is essential. If we are going to get along with God, it is essential. If we are going to get along with each other, it is essential.

❖ ❖ ❖ ❖ ❖
Forgiveness holds a family together. It is essential. It holds a church together. It is essential. It holds the Kingdom of God together. It is essential. Why is that so? Why is it more important for us to be forgiving than for us to stand in judgment? Does that mean that "anything goes"? Once again address the issues of being forgiving and permissiveness.

What roles do the Law (recognizing and condemning sin) and the Gospel (the message of God's grace) play in all of this?

Now let me tell you how that works itself out in my life. I'll be the first to admit that I am not all that great as a husband and father. My wife probably could have done better. As for my children, they had no choice in the matter. My friends, when I was growing up, warned me about this. They said that I would not be easy to live with. There are others whom I know who seem to have a lot more talent and personality and compassion and charm and all of those other good qualities than I do. My wife and children see most of my foibles and follies and sins. I have little to stand on. There is little evidence by which I can plead my innocence. Nevertheless, in spite of all of this, we are a family, and we have stayed together as a family. To what can that be attributed? To one simple fact: We are all willing to forgive each other. That forgiving is hard to do sometimes. It is often hard to pull it off. But we stand tall in each other's company, because by Christ we have been forgiven, and in Him we can do the same for each other.

It has been said that it is easier to love (and forgive) at a distance than close at hand, and that it is easier to love and forgive someone you don't know than it is to forgive someone whom you do know. Why do you think that is so? Is it true that the closer a person is to you the more difficult it is to forgive that person? What are some of the things that stand in the way of you forgiving the members of your family? Do you have any family traditions that help you to forgive each other?

Sometimes the words of the Confession and Forgiveness which are part of the worship service are so routine that they are in danger of losing their meaning. What might be a way in which those words could be made to be more meaningful?

The wonderful thing about such forgiveness is that it is so complete. That makes it completely unnecessary for any of us to keep score. Which reminds me of what the disciples asked Jesus: "How many times should we forgive? Seven?" Today we might even cut that in half: "Three strikes and you're out. After all, there have to be limits." No! There do not have to be limits! There are none with God. He is infinitely gracious and generous in His forgiving us. His forgiveness is

"Fool me once, shame on you. Fool me twice, shame on me. Fool me three times and...." How is that way of thinking different than Kingdom thinking? How is it different than that for which we pray in the Fifth Petition?

seven times seventy. That is very much, and, quite frankly, I find it hard to live up to that. But that is why I constantly need to pray both ends of this petition: "Lord, forgive me for sinning against you and my neighbors, against my wife and children. Now give me the mind to be as forgiving with them, all of them, as you have been with me." That does not come easily. "So, Lord, teach us to pray and live that kind of Kingdom life."

Questions

1. What happens if and when the garbage is not "taken out"?

2. How is what the one soldier did for the other one a parallel to what Jesus did for us?

3. Is our being forgiven conditioned upon us being forgiving, or is our being forgiving conditioned upon our being forgiven?

4. What does the completeness of forgiveness make unnecessary?

Discussion

1. Discuss why the Fifth Petition is the "heart and soul" of the Lord's Prayer. If there is no forgiveness, of what also can there be none?

2. Discuss ways in which sin unforgiven hinders Kingdom living.

The Lord's Prayer
The Sixth Petition

❖ ❖ ❖ ❖ ❖

There are a lot of distractions in life. In fact each moment of each day we are bombarded with hundreds of different signals, all of which seek to get our attention. Take a minute and try to list as many signals that are coming to you right now from your surroundings (i.e., people talking, noise in the air, and so forth) and as many as you can identify that are coming right now from within you (i.e., you're hungry, there is something else on your mind). Are these signals good or bad? Can they be one or the other, depending upon the circumstance? Identify what might be the factor that makes a signal that calls for your attention either good or bad.

The devil always uses these signals as diversionary tactics. Discuss an example of that. From what is he trying to divert your attention?

❖ ❖ ❖ ❖ ❖

The Kingdom Prayer continues: "And lead us not into temptation."

But God doesn't tempt anyone to sin, does He? Whoever heard of such a thing? Therefore, why should we even have to pray such a prayer as this one?

Martin Luther himself asked, "What does this mean?" that we should pray "lead us not into temptation." As always, he also answered his own question.

> *God tempts no one. We pray in this petition that God would guard and keep us so that the devil, the world, and our sinful nature may not deceive us or mislead us into false belief, despair, and other great shame and vice. Although we are attached by these things, we pray that we may finally overcome them and win the victory.*

Some interpreters of the Greek language, the language in which the Bible was originally written, and in which we have the Lord's Prayer recorded by the Evangelists Matthew and Luke, tell us that this Sixth Petition can also be translated as, "Save us in the time of trial." I think that translation does a good job in catching just what it was that Jesus was saying to His disciples when He said these words as part of His response to their request, "Lord, teach us to pray."

You see, there is a real danger to a Christian that in a time of trial (a time of testing, when pressures are great, when things go badly, when he or she might be the object of insult and/or ridicule, when not only faith but also faithfulness is being questioned) both the faith and faithfulness might be abandoned. That is the time of temptation.

Pressures to be faithless to the Faith are plentiful. Identify some of the pressures that were brought to bear upon people throughout the history of the Christian Church. What are some of the pressures being brought to bear upon Christians in your community today? From where do these pressures come? Are these the same kinds of pressures that are being brought to bear upon you?

This prayer was taught by Jesus to a group of disciples all of whom would not only be persecuted for the faith, but also all of whom (except one, John, and, of course, Judas Iscariot) would be martyred (executed) because they both believed in and were faithful to Jesus. Therefore, Jesus taught them this petition, this prayer, in which they would be asking not for an escape when persecution came their way, but in which they would be asking that they would not abandon the faith and their faithfulness under such pressures. The pressures which many of those early Christians endured, their time of trial, their temptations, came from members of their own families, from their countrymen, from the hostile Roman government, and from their own doubts.

"Lord, help us not to break under such pressure!"

Martin Luther picked up on this when he wrote in the explanation to the Sixth Petition that here we pray that "the devil, the world, and our sinful nature may not deceive us or mislead us into false belief, despair, and other great shame and vice." The greatest of all shame and vice is unfaithfulness to the Lord Jesus.

I have not personally been persecuted because I am a Christian. When I was young and growing up in my hometown, my friends, even though they were not known around town as being model acolytes and altar boys, didn't even tease me because I was going to study to become a minister. The simple fact is that I cannot point to any time when my life was threatened because I confessed Jesus Christ as Savior. I also doubt that there are many of you who can recall any time when your life was threatened because you believed in Jesus. Therefore, it would seem that the situation facing the early Christians is much different than anything we face today. Talking about Christians being thrown to the lions in the Roman Coliseum or about saints being burned at the stake simply does not speak to our situations in life. Yes, there are some people in some parts of the world who really do face persecution and possible death because of the faith, but that is not us. So perhaps this petition, "Lead us not into temptation," or "Deliver us in the time of trouble," simply doesn't mean what it once did.

❖ ❖ ❖ ❖ ❖
Some say that the greatest temptation that the devil can place before someone is the temptation to despair, to become discouraged, to give up, to lead one into despondency. Do you think that is so? Why is despair so dangerous, so deadly, for the Christian?
❖ ❖ ❖ ❖ ❖

Wrong! It does. There are many ways in which our faith and our faithfulness are also assaulted. For example, I am a pastor. When things don't go right, when I become frustrated because the people of the congregation I serve just are not responding the way I think that they should (indeed, when some don't seem to be responding at all), when I see them behaving in ways which are not becoming of Christians, I have the tendency to get discouraged, maybe even depressed, and wonder, "Is it worth it? Is having faith in Jesus and being faithful to Him really worth it? Is it worth all the effort?"

And then there are those times when things in my life go badly. Perhaps a disease or some tragedy or some disaster strikes close to home. Then I might even wonder and say, "God, if there is a god, why don't you do something about this? Why don't you help?" That is when my faith is in its time of trial. That is when I am being tempted to give up. That is when I might not feel much like praying at all at that time.

❖ ❖ ❖ ❖ ❖
Another word for "trial" is "testing." A time of trial is a time of testing. Testing serves as something far more than just trying to trip someone up. Testing can also serve the purpose of strengthening. Steel is tested; it is put through a time of trial. It is tempered: pounded and hammered so that its impurities are beaten out of it and it can stand greater stress. Do you think that sometimes we are tested by God for much the same reason?

However, even though we are tested, we pray that we do not break, that we don't fall victim to a time of testing and trial, so that temptation doesn't have its way with us. Give an example of this process.
❖ ❖ ❖ ❖ ❖

I don't know how your faith gets assaulted. I'm not now referring to all the petty vices that present themselves to you. We are talking about something more than little annoyances. After all, even the greatest of saints had their problems. Many a fine prophet took more than just a little nip every now and then. Many a noble man of God has been known to lose his temper and to season his vocabulary with words that should not even be mentioned among us. Not just a few saints had an eye for a pretty girl or a handsome man. No one, no matter how much he or she is admired, is exempt from these petty vices. We all fall victim to a wide assortment of temptations. And from these temptations we too need to be delivered before they do to us too much damage. But something more is involved here. What is at stake is not just some little slip or the other. What is at stake here is the whole faith; what is at stake here is discipleship itself.

What we pray for in the Sixth Petition is that under pressure, under any circumstance, we would not toss in the towel on the whole business, the whole Kingdom business. We pray that we would not give up on the faith and on our faithfulness.

❖ ❖ ❖ ❖ ❖
What are some of the subtle ways in which the devil picks at your faith and faithfulness?
❖ ❖ ❖ ❖ ❖

The direct assaults on our faith are easy to recognize. The subtle tests and temptations are, however, the really dangerous ones. For example, no one has ever held a gun to my head and said, "Deny the faith." My life has never been threatened because I am a Christian. Nobody has ever made fun of me because I am a Christian. But the devil knows of subtle ways to work on me. As I mentioned before, when things don't go right, when I am disappointed or frustrated, or when sad things or things which I don't always understand happen, then I have the tendency to drift, to drift away from the faith; and that is when I have the tendency to become a bit on the faithless side.

As far as the faith is concerned, those moments have a depressing effect. When a person feels depressed the last thing in the world that he or she wants to do is to do "anything." Depression makes you want to just sit there, and yet that is the worst thing in the world to do — to do nothing. The best thing would be to get up and get moving. Then you would feel better again. In fact, much depression comes exactly from doing nothing, and the less you do, the worse it gets. Thus, when a person is growing cold as far as the faith and faithfulness are concerned, when faith living is becoming depressed, when Kingdom living is being ignored, the hardest thing in the world to do is to do anything at all. So faith and faithfulness grow colder and colder. And that is precisely why it is important for us to pray this petition faithfully. We pray, even when we don't feel like praying, that God would come to us and deliver us from our faithlessness.

❖ ❖ ❖ ❖ ❖
Do you think that it is hypocritical to pray when you don't feel like praying, or when perhaps you don't even mean what you are praying? What might be a good reason for praying even when you don't feel like it? Is going to church something like that? Do you feel that there is value in going to church even when you don't feel like going? What good could possibly come out of going through the motions even though your heart might not be in it?
❖ ❖ ❖ ❖ ❖

One of the best ways in which God has provided for us, and one of the best ways in which He answers our Sixth Petition, is by providing for us the company of other Christians. Members of the family of faith, members of the congregations to which we belong, are among our best defenses "in the time of trial." They are our best defense not just when they have something encouraging to say or give to us, but, and perhaps even more importantly, they are our best defense when we have the opportunity to say something encouraging and to minister to them even when we might not feel much like doing it.

❖ ❖ ❖ ❖ ❖
It has been said that "idleness is the devil's workshop." It might also be said that "loneliness is also a time for the devil to be busy." Why do you think that might be so? Do you think that the company of other Christians is important for a person to stay strong in the faith? Refer to Galatians 6:2. Apply this Bible passage to this sort of situation.
❖ ❖ ❖ ❖ ❖

I have found this to be true in my own life. I get down in the spirit just as much as anybody else. I even get depressed as far as my faith is concerned. And I am tempted to become faithless, to slack off in my discipleship. But because I am a minister, a pastor, I have many opportunities to share God's word of hope, of courage, of forgiveness with others. There are even times when I have those opportunities and my heart is not in it. Yet, as I speak the word, for example, in Bible class or at some hospital bedside, or even as I work preparing another chapter of this book, I find that the Holy Spirit seems to be at work within me. He gets through to me, and I find then that the tables are once again being turned on the old devil who thought that he had me in his grasp.

❖ ❖ ❖ ❖ ❖
It is said that "in giving there is receiving." That means that the person who gives gets back an abundant return. Have you ever experienced your faith growing stronger because you shared it with others? Try doing that.
❖ ❖ ❖ ❖ ❖

"Lord, lead us not into temptation ... Lord, save us from the time of trial. Deliver us from anything and all things which would interfere with our hallowing of Your name, which would not allow us to participate in the coming of Your Kingdom, or which would not permit us to do Your will. So give us our daily bread and everything else necessary for us to be Your Kingdom people, Your people of forgiveness and Your people who are always forgiving. Lord, we know that the temptations in life are often very serious, but, Lord, the most serious of all temptations are the temptations to give up on Kingdom living, those temptations which would have us hedge on our discipleship. Above all, deliver us from those kinds of temptations — those moments of testing." Amen.

❖ ❖ ❖ ❖ ❖

What is the greatest test of your faith that you have ever encountered? Why was it such a difficult test? After it was all over, in what condition did you find your faith? Maybe the test is not over yet. Maybe you are still right in the middle of it. If that is the case, for what would you wish? For what would you pray? The Sixth Petition?

❖ ❖ ❖ ❖ ❖

Questions

1. The words "and lead us not into temptation" can also be translated as _____.

2. Who was the only disciple who was not executed because of his faith?

3. Our petty vices are not what is meant by temptation in this petition. But what is the nature of the temptation meant here?

4. With what has God provided us for those moments when our faith gets depressed?

Discussion

1. Discuss ways in which your faith can be and often is put to the test. Include some of the pressures of the world around you.

2. Discuss some of the best ways we can "strengthen our hand" in the face of temptation.

The Lord's Prayer
The Seventh Petition

They say that there are no atheists (people who do not believe in God) in foxholes. Maybe. Maybe not. Although I have a hunch that if one doesn't believe in God when the sun is shining (at a time of peace), he probably isn't going to believe in Him when the storm breaks (at a time of war) either. Just because someone is stuck in a hole in the ground with bullets flying around overhead doesn't mean that he is going to become a believer.

An atheist is a person who says that there is no god. When might an atheist doubt that there is no god? What about that kind of situation which makes him doubt that there is no god? Do you feel closer to God, or do you feel a greater need to pray when you are faced with critical or life-and-death situations? What is it about these situations that makes us more open to God?

Have you ever found yourself making promises to God that if He helped you, you would do some "favor" for him in return? If so, share that information with someone.

❖ ❖ ❖ ❖ ❖

The reason why they say that there are no atheists in foxholes is that when one is terrified, when one fears for his life, that supposedly puts a bit of the fear of God into him. Thus, he who is now so terrified will quickly fall onto his knees (if, indeed, he is not there already) and pray, "Lord, help me out of this difficult spot. And if you do, I promise to believe in you; yes, I will believe in you for the rest of my life. So, please deliver me from evil, from that which threatens to hurt and harm me."

I don't want to argue about foxholes and terrified soldiers, but I would like to talk about this last petition of that prayer which Jesus' disciples asked Him to teach them. I would like to focus on just what it means when we petition, "Deliver us from evil."

Is it not true that we often find ourselves in peculiar fixes, in hot spots, in trouble, in some sort of foxhole or the other? Some of these moments might even be life-threatening. Therefore, frequently in panic, we look, we beg, for help, for deliverance. We must face the fact that many of these problems which harass us are bigger than we are. So we turn to Him who, we have been taught, is bigger than us all. We pray to God, saying, "Help me, God; deliver me from this evil."

That, however, is not what the Seventh Petition is really all about. It is not prayer just for foxholes, a prayer designed to be prayed in those moments when we feel that we are under fire. It is not some sort of magical formula to be recited when we feel ourselves pinned up against a wall or down in a hole. It is not an SOS to some divine "Lone Ranger" who will come riding to our rescue from beyond the horizon, and who, once his mission has been accomplished, will disappear again, not to return until He finds us in trouble once more.

Can you take the prayer "deliver us from evil" and appropriate it to the entire business of Kingdom living? In other words, can you see how this prayer is concerned about a lot more than just momentary deliverance from some sort of evil or difficult situation? By now have you begun to see that the entire Lord's Prayer is concerned about a lot more than just day-to-day problems and difficulties? It's about the whole kingdom!

The concern of the Seventh Petition, like the concern of all the other petitions of this disciples' prayer, has to do with the Kingdom, the whole Kingdom, its welfare and our being a part of it. It is not principally concerned with private calls for help. It is far more public than that.

Look at it this way:

> *God, may your name be holy as we carry your reputation,*
> *being part of the coming of your Kingdom,*
> *doing your will.*
> *So give us our daily bread so that we might be strengthened for the task.*
> *Move our hearts to be forgiving toward others as you have been forgiving toward us, for such is the way of Kingdom living.*

*Give us strength for the time of trial,
and, finally, give us victory over the evil
one who constantly seeks to destroy your
Kingdom and our being a part of it.*

In that last petition we are publicly asking God that when the devil comes, and we take our licks from him, that then He, God, would help us to win the victory over him, so that all the other Kingdom things for which we have prayed might be fulfilled.

❖ ❖ ❖ ❖ ❖

Review for yourself and put into your own words the six previous Kingdom things for which we have prayed in the first six petitions.

❖ ❖ ❖ ❖ ❖

Some translations of Matthew 6:13, that verse from the Sermon on the Mount which contains our Seventh Petition, translate the words "Deliver us from evil" as "Save us from the evil one." The implication is that evil is not just some impersonal condition (like having the flu), but it is a personal force. In other words, there is no evil without "someone" being behind it. Evil is not an inorganic, lifeless, inanimate object. Evil is always willed. It is alive. It doesn't just happen. It is caused.

Thanks to television and the movies, the devil and the forces of evil are presented these days as being nothing more than fiendish freaks. So freakish are they that we can hardly take them seriously anymore. They are there for our amusement. They scare us, and then we laugh away any sense of their reality. We giggle and admit that they are fake.

Evil can not be impersonal. It is always personal. If that is so can we ever say that a person is not responsible for his or her behavior? Can the sin be separated from the sinner? Can we ever say, "I can hate the sin but not the sinner"? Can evil ever not be associated with some being or the other? Can there be evil without the "Evil One"?

Even though evil thrives in certain circumstances, can it ever be blamed on the genes or on the environment? What contributing factors do the genes or the environment make toward evil behavior?

What effect do you think the portraying of evil and acts of evil in the media (especially television and the movies) has on society? Does it contribute to the creating of a more evil society? Can the media (especially television and movies) make a positive contribution to the quality of a society? If you were a film or program producer, what kind of programs would you produce?

❖ ❖ ❖ ❖ ❖

The evil one referred to in the Seventh Petition, however, is not to be taken so lightly. Yes, there are all sorts of evil in the world and they must be taken seriously: murder, rape, robbery, molestation, terrorism, drug abuse, pornography, and so on. Yes, there is all sort of evil around. And it is not just a condition. We can not just attribute it to the environment. We must not treat evil as an "it." No, it must be taken personally. We must realize that evil is a "he" or a "she" or maybe even a "me."

I don't know if we can limit evil to a "he" or a "she" or a "you" or a "me," but this I do know: When we refer to it as an impersonal condition rather than a personal force, we are beginning not to take him or her as seriously as we ought. That's when she or he is getting ready to raise all kinds of hell with us. Therefore, we should not consider the devil to be something like the wind. Instead, the devil is a being with whom we must reckon, especially when he or she has her or his way with you and with me.

That is why Saint Paul advises all those who would be of the family of faith, all those who would choose to be disciples of Jesus, to put on the whole armor of God so that we can do battle against the wiles (the will) of the devil (Ephesians 6:10). The devil is a formidable enemy, and he is not to be taken lightly. The words which end the prayer the disciples asked their Lord to teach them, "Deliver us from evil," are a battle cry. The enemy is not a pushover. We must take the devil seriously. She/he is a formidable foe against whom we must do constant battle. Yes, the Seventh Petition is a battle cry not merely a part of a lullaby (the Lord's Prayer) to be sung at weddings and funerals.

If the devil, the source of all evil, is really a formidable enemy, what can you do to battle against him/her? Look at Ephesians 6:10-20. Identify in your own terms the following pieces of equipment: the armor of God; the belt of truth; the breastplate of righteousness; the boots of peace; the shield of faith; the helmet of salvation; and the sword of the Spirit. Also, what does it mean to pray in the Spirit? What do you think would be a Spirit-driven prayer? Do you think that the Lord's Prayer can qualify as a Spirit-driven prayer?

❖ ❖ ❖ ❖ ❖

Finally, the Lord's Prayer concludes with a resounding "Amen." The word "Amen" is a word of sureness. It rings with certainty, with confidence. Martin Luther said that this word "is nothing else than an unquestioning affirmation of faith on the part of the person who uses it." There is no room for doubt here. We don't say, "If you be so pleased, God, answer, these petitions." Praying like that would be an insult to God. He, Himself, through His Son Jesus taught us to pray with much more assertiveness than that.

> *... I should be certain that these petitions are pleasing to our Father in heaven, and are heard by Him; for He Himself has commanded us to pray in this way and has promised to hear us. Amen, amen means, "Yes, yes, it shall be so."*

❖ ❖ ❖ ❖ ❖
Does the "Amen" at the end of the Lord's Prayer signify that those who have prayed it really want and expect its petitions to be answered? If the seven prayers of this one prayer are all answered for you, what effect will that have on your life? Will it alter your behavior? If so, how?
❖ ❖ ❖ ❖ ❖

Saint James writes in the first chapter of his letter, "Ask in faith, with no doubting, for he who doubts is like a wave of the sea that is driven and tossed by the wind. For that person must not suppose that a double-minded man, unstable in all his ways, will receive anything from the Lord" (James 1:6-8).

Therefore, let us not forget that this prayer, with all its separate seven prayers, is a prayer which Jesus Himself taught to his disciples in response to their asking, "Lord, teach us to pray." He responded to their request. However, in that response I don't think He meant to say, "Here is a good example of a prayer which might work sometimes." No! Absolutely not! Instead, here is a prayer which is to be boldly put before the throne of the Almighty. No doubting allowed! No vacillating back and forth permitted! No saying, "Well, God, you probably won't answer these petitions anyway, but it can't hurt to ask. After all, nothing ventured, nothing gained." Again, No! A thousand times NO!

❖ ❖ ❖ ❖ ❖
"He who hesitates is lost." Doubting is like hesitating. What opportunities have you missed because you doubted or hesitated? What is at risk when doubting that God will answer these seven prayers?
❖ ❖ ❖ ❖ ❖

This is the prayer of the Kingdom. In it we ask for the whole thing. So pray always to the Father who is in heaven.

Again, and again, I say, "AMEN."

Questions

1. What do we often promise God if He will only get us out of a difficult spot?

2. The evil from which we pray to be delivered in this petition is not some impersonal force but _____.

3. When we use the word "amen" at the end of the Lord's Prayer, for what are we leaving no room?

4. For what are we praying in the Lord's Prayer?

Discussion

1. Discuss some of the ways in which evil manifests itself in personal ways in your life and in the world around you. (Perhaps you might also refer to evil which sometimes is "in" you.)

2. Discuss the issue of "certainty" with regards to this Kingdom Prayer.

3. What are appropriate times, places, and occasions for a good and wholesome and God-pleasing use of this prayer?

www.ingramcontent.com/pod-product-compliance
Lightning Source LLC
Chambersburg PA
CBHW081218230426
43666CB00015B/2786